LESSONS FOR LITERACY

Lessons
for Literacy
PROMOTING PRESCHOOL SUCCESS

Harlan S. Hansen, PhD, and Ruth M. Hansen, PhD

Redleaf Press®
www.redleafpress.org
800-423-8309

KH

Published by Redleaf Press
10 Yorkton Court
St. Paul, MN 55117
www.redleafpress.org

First edition 2010
Cover design by Erin New
Interior typeset in Berkeley Oldstyle
Photos on pages 57, 59, 70, and 164 courtesy of the authors
Photos on pages 46, 47, 48, 58, 60, 61, 64, 65, 124 (lower left), and 155 courtesy of Handrigan Design
Photo on page 68 courtesy of Steve Wewerka
Photos on page 72 courtesy of Greg Thompson
Illustrations on pages 56, 62, 63, 83, 184, 186, 190, 191, and 192 courtesy of Elizabeth Bub
Thanks to Chrissie Mahaffy and Nina LeSaout of Greenspoon Child Care, Minneapolis,
   for the name-sticks on page 60
Developmental edit by Deanne Kells
Printed in the United States of America
16 15 14 13 12 11 10 09   1 2 3 4 5 6 7 8

Library of Congress Cataloging-in-Publication Data

Hansen, Harlan S.
 Lessons for literacy : promoting preschool success / Harlan S. Hansen, and Ruth M. Hansen. — 1st ed.
   p. cm.
 ISBN 978-1-933653-90-7
 1. Language arts (Preschool) 2. Education, Preschool—Activity programs. I. Hansen, Ruth M. II. Title.
 LB1140.5.L3H36 2009
 372.6—dc22
              2009001051

Printed on acid-free paper

1/21/11

This book is dedicated to our grandchildren, Laura, Scott, Chris, Lauder, and Jack, and to their children, and their children, and their children . . .

And to all teachers of young children, who are asked to do so much and are given so few resources to meet the challenge.

And in memory of Professors David and Madeline Davis, who taught us so much about children and what they need to understand and who, way back then, had the foresight to bring us together as a couple.

LESSONS FOR LITERACY

ACKNOWLEDGMENTS   xi

INTRODUCTION   1
Historical Overview: Changing Beliefs about Preschool Literacy 1
Stages of Reading 3
Program History and Focus 3
Strategies to Promote Positive Literacy Development 5

ASSESSMENT   11
Individual Profile (Four- and Five-Year-Olds) 14
Group Profile 15
Periodic Assessment Tool 18
Writing Anecdotal Reports 45
Portfolios 47
A Note about Three-Year-Olds 49
Individual Profile (Three-Year-Olds) 50

CLASSROOM ESSENTIALS   53
Two Foundations 53
Twenty-One Classroom Essentials 54
    Effective Calendars 55
    An I'll Wait Timeline 57
    News Bulletin Boards 58
    Teacher Photos 59
    Individual Attendance Devices 60
    Super Star of the Week 61
    Data-Collecting Activities 62
    Language Experience Stories 63
    Yearlong Birthday Calendar 64
    Helpers Charts 65
    Words in the Environment 66
    Song Charts 67
    Alphabet and Number Charts 67
    Literacy Centers 68
    Labeled Bulletin Boards 69
    Writing Materials 69
    Word Walls 70
    Maps 71
    Comfortable Group Meeting Areas 72
    Classroom Centers 73
    Field Trips and Resource People 74

MUSIC OF LITERACY 77

The Importance of Music for Literacy Development 77
The Use of Music in Early Childhood Programs 78
The Value of Song Charts 80
Introducing a New Song 80
Where to Find Music for Early Childhood Programs 81
    "Hush, Little Baby" 83
    "Pretty Colors" 85
    "Who Is Wearing . . . ?" 86
    "If You Are Wearing . . ." 87
    "This Old Man" 88
    "Ten in the Bed" 89
    "Ten Little Sailors" 90
    "Head and Shoulders, Knees and Toes" 91
    "The Hokey Pokey" 92
    "The Alphabet Song" 93
    "B-I-N-G-O" 94
    "Old MacDonald Had a Farm" 95
    "Itsy, Bitsy Spider" 96

CONNECTING WITH THE HOME 99

Successful Strategies for Working with Families 99
Sample Family Letter 103

LESSON ACTIVITIES 107

Lesson Activity 1: Knows first and last name 108
Lesson Activity 2: Writes first name and first letter of last name 111
Lesson Activity 3: Repeats home address 113
Lesson Activity 4: Knows purpose of and can dial 911 115
Lesson Activity 5: Recognizes eleven basic colors 117
Lesson Activity 6: Counts from 1 to 31 120
Lesson Activity 7: Recognizes numerals 1 to 10 out of order 122
Lesson Activity 8: Demonstrates an understanding of one-to-one correspondence 125
Lesson Activity 9: Recites the alphabet 127
Lesson Activity 10: Identifies at least ten uppercase letters out of order
    Identifies at least ten lowercase letters out of order 128
Lesson Activity 11: Recognizes and names a square, circle, rectangle, and triangle 130
Lesson Activity 12: Copies a square, circle, rectangle, and triangle 133
Lesson Activity 13: Identifies basic body parts 134
Lesson Activity 14: Reproduces basic body parts when drawing a person 136
Lesson Activity 15: Demonstrates appropriate cutting skills 138
Lesson Activity 16: Demonstrates appropriate pasting skills 140

Lesson Activity 17: Understands the concept of print: Knows the difference between a letter, a word, and a sentence

Understands the concept of print: Knows that print goes left to right and top to bottom with a return sweep

Understands the concept of print: Knows that print tells the story and illustrations help tell the story 141

Lesson Activity 18: Understands the concept of a story: Knows that an author writes the story

Understands the concept of a story: Knows that an illustrator creates the pictures

Understands the concept of a story: Knows that a story has a beginning, a middle, and an end

Understands the concept of a story: Knows there are different characters in a story

Understands the concept of a story: Knows the story has a setting where it takes place

Understands the concept of a story: Knows that a conversation might take place 143

Lesson Activity 19: Predicts what comes next in a story 145

Lesson Activity 20: Retells a story with sufficient details 146

Lesson Activity 21: Differentiates and reproduces rhyming sounds 148

Lesson Activity 22: Differentiates and reproduces beginning sounds 149

Lesson Activity 23: Shows growth in writing alphabet and picture code systems 151

Lesson Activity 24: Reads simple stories using pictures and/or words 154

Lesson Activity 25: Shows growth in vocabulary and language use 156

Lesson Activity 26: Identifies common words found inside and outside the classroom 158

Lesson Activity 27: Understands and uses comparative terms 159

Lesson Activity 28: Shows initiative in engaging in simple reading and writing activities 161

Journal Writing 162

APPENDIX   167

Blackline Masters 167

Tips for Families to Encourage Positive Reading Behaviors

Family Letter

Name Sheet (Lesson Activity 10)

Dot-to-Dot Shapes (Lesson Activity 12)

Fix the Doll (Lesson Activity 13)

Shapes to Cut Out (Lesson Activity 15)

Cutting Lines (Lesson Activity 15)

Cutting a Spiral (Lesson Activity 15)

Folding a Hat (Lesson Activity 15)

Folding a Cup (Lesson Activity 15)

Shapes to Paste (Lesson Activity 16)

Beginning, Middle, End (Lesson Activity 18)

Stages of Writing (Journal Writing)

Milestones for Three- and Four-Year-Olds

I'll Wait Timeline

Acknowledgments

We wish to acknowledge the following people for their invaluable assistance to us throughout the writing of this book.

Shannah Gillespie, Rosario "Charo" Brueggen, and Barb Schoenbeck, who provided concrete examples of activities for young children.

Jean McKeel and Frannie Kain, who gave positive direction to the first draft of the manuscript.

Mary Hertogs, for her photographs.

The directors and teachers of Kiddie Korral and Cubbie Bear Learning Center, who allowed us to demonstrate that teachers of young children can effectively involve young children in the development of literacy outcomes by using developmentally appropriate practices.

Myra Shapiro and the Naples Alliance for Children, who provided the organizational framework and encouragement for our work in Southwest Florida.

The Community Foundation of Naples, who provided funding for a study that became the basis for this book.

Deanne Kells, who combined her strong background in early childhood education with her excellent editing skills to make these ideas useful to all teachers of young children.

David Heath, editor-in-chief of Redleaf Press, who not only did a fine job of coordinating the writing and production of this book but also contributed through his love for the music of young children.

Jim Handrigan, creative director of Redleaf Press, who provided exceptional design work and graphics to bring the book to life.

Introduction

Historical Overview: Changing Beliefs about Preschool Literacy

Prior to the 1970s, kindergarten and prekindergarten programs rarely included literacy skills. Most practitioners based their decisions in this area on the belief—supported by the work of the Gesell Institute of Child Development—that literacy development was a product of maturation. Following their observations of children, researchers at Gesell declared that children were not ready to begin the study of reading until as late as age eight (http://school.familyeducation.com/home-school/reading/38692.html). This meant that the purpose of early childhood programs was to allow children to follow their own interests through involvement in various centers: blocks, housekeeping, dress up, art, puzzles, games, music, nature, and so on. In fact, any activity that was seen as related to reading was negatively referred to as "prereading" or "reading readiness." Group activities included reading stories, singing, and some basic movement development. Focusing on social development was the accepted standard.

Starting in the early 1970s, and most probably based on the work of Benjamin Bloom and the soon-to-follow Head Start programs, the idea of "getting them early" pushed the literacy focus to curriculum programs in kindergarten. Many schools' districts purchased reading programs that included a kindergarten component, usually considered the "readiness phase," endeavoring to get children ready for the first-grade program.

This created a serious debate among educators. Early childhood professional organizations challenged the inclusion of such programs, especially the use of workbooks. Kindergarten teachers, long trained in the social development approach to instruction, felt that their professional judgments were being called into question. On the other hand, curriculum directors, wanting to satisfy the demands of first-grade teachers and involved families, pressed on with reading program adoptions.

This caused a backlash in preschool programs. The notion that literacy activities might now be included in the preschool curriculum was cast in a negative light. Rather than examining how literacy skills might best be included for four-year-olds, teachers reacted mainly against the way these skills were often being taught at the kindergarten level. Here's how the argument went: "If worksheets are inappropriate for kindergarten children, their inclusion in preschool programs will be devastating." Except in some preschool programs that advertised themselves as including the teaching of reading, the vast majority of early childhood programs continued on with their traditional programs.

The real entry of literacy skills into preschool programs happened as a result of several factors. Sesame Street, with its emphasis on the alphabet and language development, brought literacy skills into the home. Head Start programs began to include basic skills. A new breed of parents and families realized that their children could be involved in literacy skills at a younger age than they had assumed. Finally, public kindergartens felt the pressures of teaching to a wide range of individual differences within the traditional group-oriented curricula. This called for two approaches: either holding some children back until they were "ready" for kindergarten or asking preschool teachers to begin including basic literacy skills in the four-year-old curriculum.

In the later 1990s and early 2000s, with the growing emphasis on integrated language-arts programs in professional writings and textbooks, the development of literacy skills found a legitimate place in prekindergarten programs. The idea was that basic and literacy skills could be introduced through authentic activities while being adapted to each child's level of ability and learning style.

However, recognizing that preschools could now be involved in activities that help children be successful in later school programs has not changed the face of early childhood programs. Much of the training needed to implement such an approach has not been made available to preschool teachers. Rapid turnover in the field has further clouded the issue. Some programs have resorted to published curricula with their worksheet approach commonly found in kindergarten. As for the emerging curricula, written especially for preschool programs, most are organized in such a way that it is difficult for untrained teachers to understand and make the best use of the material.

Stages of Reading

Children evolve through several stages as they learn to read: emergent, beginning, developing, and independent. Most three- and four-year-olds are in the emergent stage. This stage includes mastery of concepts, behaviors, and skills that prepare children for the next stages, which highlight actual reading and writing skills.

The literacy activities presented in this manual are developmentally appropriate for children in the emergent stage of reading.

Basic to any skill development for emergent readers are these understandings:

- Print has meaning and function.
- Illustrations aid in telling a story.
- Print is made up of letters, words, sentences, and paragraphs.
- Reading progresses from left to right and top to bottom on the page.
- Letters and words have sounds that help the reader decode meaning.

Activities to promote these understandings and related skills are included throughout the book.

Program History and Focus

It is the current response of preschools across America to the changing beliefs about preschool literacy that has led to this book. The purpose of this publication is to assist all preschool teachers to know

- the outcomes that should be aimed for to best prepare young children to become readers;
- how to assess children's progress and adapt literacy instruction to their needs;
- how to select literacy activities that integrate into the existing curriculum.

This book was developed over time and with great care and effort. It began with our desire to remain active in early childhood education after leaving our academic careers. Once we decided on Naples, Florida, as our winter residence, we set out to find the best opportunities for volunteerism to benefit young children. We attended several fund-raisers for young children's projects and were soon contacted by Myra Shapiro, president of the Naples Alliance for Children.

We were invited to join the Apple Blossom Committee to select the top preschool teachers in Collier County. This Florida county includes the town of Immokalee, which has a large migrant population. On our visits to observe nominees, we discovered that there were many preschools serving children of low-income families.

One of the needs we perceived was that programs lacked written outcomes for their teachers to follow. Lack of formal training for the teachers, frequent staff turnover, and little on-the-job assistance resulted in programs consisting of random activities on one hand or didactic skills programs on the other. To help solve this problem, we applied for and received a small grant to write outcomes for each age group from infants through four-year-olds. We also developed a recording system to monitor children's progress. The grant provided funds for free workshops for teachers in the county, a copy of the outcomes and recording instrument for each site, and a follow-up consultation in their centers.

We also noted that teachers needed assistance in handling behavior problems. Working with colleagues, we received another small grant that resulted in The Discipline Toolbox, a teacher-oriented resource for addressing forty common behavior problems in a developmentally appropriate manner. This booklet was provided free of charge to all preschool teachers in the county.

At the same time these issues were being addressed, the preparation of children for kindergarten was a major concern in the Collier County schools (reflecting what was true across the country). This concern in Collier County started a movement toward establishing formal prereading programs that were not developmentally appropriate.

To counter that movement, we applied for and received a large grant from the Naples Community Foundation to conduct a study to see if preschool teachers could be trained to better prepare four-year-old children for kindergarten in a developmentally appropriate manner. We selected two low-income preschool programs in the area and assessed the programs' current groups of children to serve as a comparison group. Over the next two years, we identified literacy outcomes, developed an assessment tool, and worked with the teachers on appropriate assessment and classroom activities. We considered the first year a training year and the second year the basis for the study. At the end of that time, the children were assessed using the same instrument as the comparison group. The study group showed statistically significant gains over the scores of the comparison group on twenty of the twenty-eight items measured.

We then documented some of the activities that were appropriate for the outcomes, put them together into a book, and used the remaining grant money to publish a skeleton version of the program. Free workshops were again provided to preschool teachers in the area, and everyone received a free copy of the book.

Ultimately, we submitted our manuscript to Redleaf Press, and were enthusiastically encouraged to expand the materials into a comprehensive program. *Lessons for Literacy* is the result of that effort.

Strategies to Promote Positive Literacy Development

Some fundamental activities occur in classrooms that promote literacy development. As teachers plan their environments, teaching strategies, and classroom time, these fundamentals should remain at the forefront:

- Nurture print awareness.
- Establish a library center.
- Read aloud to children every day.
- Provide shared book experiences.
- Provide opportunities for choral reading.
- Provide opportunities for functional reading.
- Provide opportunities for children to write.
- Engage children in meaningful conversations.
- Help connect in-class literacy experiences to the home and the community.
- Be intentional when referring to early reading and writing.
- Conduct authentic assessments of literacy experiences.

Nurture Print Awareness

Provide a print-rich environment where children can see reading and writing as useful and themselves as competent communicators. For example, you can include

- individual check-in devices with children's names;
- signs labeling objects in the room;
- a news bulletin board;
- a classroom helpers chart;
- directional signs;
- labeled bulletin boards that give written clues to their content (for example, "Our Yarn and Glue Creations").

Establish a Library Center

Make the library center inviting through the use of comfortable chairs, tables, throw rugs, and pillows. Include a variety of books to satisfy varying interests. Display posters of books, which are easily obtained from libraries or local bookstores. Include media devices that make it easy for children to listen to stories.

Read Aloud to Children Every Day

Reading to children serves three important purposes:

1. It is enjoyable. Read one storybook-style text every day so children will experience the sheer pleasure of hearing a book read from cover to cover. Once you select the book, set the stage for reading it aloud. Introduce the book and bring it to life through varied forms of presentation. Do not follow up with questions. Let the children enjoy the story as they hear it.
2. It informs. Whenever appropriate, read children nonfiction books that provide specific information related to some topic under study or of high interest to the children. Ask questions to make sure they understand the information.
3. It teaches literacy. Read books that involve children in basic literacy activities related to the literacy outcomes. Follow up with questions and discussions of concepts of print, rhyming, retelling, and language development.

Provide Shared Book Experiences

Actively involve the children in reading:

*   Read along.
*   Read aloud to the group.
*   Read to individuals.

Allow time for children to read the pictures of a book or to retell stories to the class or to their friends. Set aside some regular time when children can browse through books.

Provide Opportunities for Choral Reading

Plan large-group readings of familiar written literature (fingerplays, nursery rhymes, poems, songs, stories, and so on). Also encourage small groups to practice and then read to the entire class. Allow the groups to read their works to children in other classrooms.

Provide Opportunities for Functional Reading

Include written information in your classroom such as

- a calendar of events;
- recipes for food preparation;
- bulletin-board displays;
- directions for completing helpers' jobs;
- word cards naming objects around the classroom, at home, in the hallways, and in the neighborhood.

Provide Opportunities for Children to Write

Set up a writing center or table stocked with various paper, magic slates, marking tools, alphabet and number charts, and so on. Encourage picture writing. Provide story starters as motivation for children to write creatively. Assist them in writing birthday cards to family members. Send cards to individuals or families highlighted in the news.

Engage Children in Meaningful Conversations

Provide time for language sharing. Children need adequate opportunities to talk about their experiences—sharing stories during sharing time, reviewing a field trip, or just talking with other children. Help them solve their disputes through oral language. Have them talk about their drawings. Encourage small-group discussions during snacktimes and lunchtimes.

Help Connect In-Class Literacy Experiences to the Home and the Community

Point out to children such things as

- family members reading newspapers, magazines, recipes, or the mail;

- family members reading and writing e-mail, sending cards, jotting down shopping or to do lists;
- community signs for safety, advertising, and addresses;
- maps and directions at public transportation stops.

Encourage families, through regular communication, to share these literacy experiences at home and to send to school some personal examples.

Be Intentional When Referring to Early Reading and Writing

Refer to book browsing or picture discussion as *reading* and random marks, scribbles, and pretend writing as *writing,* because these are legitimate forms of reading and writing. Identifying them as such helps children, early on, to identify themselves as readers and writers. Some children may still respond that they are really not reading and writing. Tell children that there are many forms of reading, and they will engage in other forms in later school years.

Conduct Authentic Assessments of Literacy Experiences

Chart children's progress over the time they are with you, and adjust your instruction as needed. Collect samples of children's works, and keep anecdotal records of children's literacy abilities and interests. Accumulate materials in a portfolio so that you can show families evidence of both accomplishments and areas that need additional development. Suggest specific ways they can work with their children at home.

PART ONE

Assessment

1

Assessment

> The goal of assessment is to document how well a child is progressing toward an outcome, not to indicate what level of growth a child should have attained.

Assessment is the process of gathering evidence to document a child's learning and growth. It helps teachers plan curriculum and instruction. It informs families so they can implement activities in the home in order to meet the needs of every child. There are two approaches to assessment: *test assessment* and *authentic assessment*.

Test assessment is periodic and identifies questions and/or tasks that are standardized to measure the progress of all students. This type of assessment is most often carried out in noninstructional settings. This form of assessment does have some shortcomings, including the following:

- Some children will be tested on days during which they may not be as attentive.
- Some children are not good test takers.
- The test items are not connected to the instruction through which the skills were learned.

Authentic assessment is distinguished by three characteristics:

1. Assessment activities are connected to real instruction. This means that children need no special preparation when the assessment takes place.
2. Assessment evaluates continual progress. This helps the teacher play an important part in all steps in learning—monitoring and adjusting what occurs in the classroom to meet children's needs.

3. Assessment takes many forms. Authentic assessment is often referred to as a *holistic approach* because it takes into consideration intellectual, social, physical, and emotional aspects of learning—all of which vary from time to time with each individual child—and this consideration is reflected in the design of various testing instruments.

This program strives to provide authentic assessment. However, a book cannot ensure what happens in the classroom. Teachers are the essential ingredient. Teachers are the ones who are there—able to observe, knowledgeable about what truly constitutes progress for each child, and using their eyes and ears (and hearts) to watch the progress children make. Nevertheless, we have attempted to provide as many tools as possible in this program. The variety of instruments suggested, described, and exemplified in this book include the following:

- **A periodic assessment tool**: This instrument is used to gather comprehensive information on children's previous learning at the start of the year and again at the middle and end of the program. This comprehensive assessment tool covers many areas of the identified curriculum and provides teachers with information on how well individuals, and the class as a whole, are progressing toward the outcomes.
- **Individual profiles of growth on program outcomes**: The Individual Profile is the key to analyzing the needs of each child and to preparing appropriate experiences suited to each child's growth and development. The Individual Profile also helps teachers share information about progress toward outcomes with other appropriate professionals and with the home.
- **A group profile to record growth on program outcomes**: The Group Profile provides a grid that summarizes the strengths and needs of the entire class so teachers can adjust and adapt instruction as needed throughout the year. The group information is pulled together from the Individual Profiles.
- **Specific information checklists**: These focus on documenting growth on parts of the curricula. Two of these checklists are included in this book: a general Child Adjustment to Environment Inventory and an Oral Language Checklist that elicits information on speech skills and children's uses of language. These are two examples of the many checklists that are available in the literature or can be constructed by a teacher to gain more specific information on children's growth.

- **Anecdotal recordings**: These are dated, informal observations that describe various areas of behaviors and progress—learning styles, learning strategies, strengths and weaknesses, or other information a teacher might want to know. Anecdotal recordings are used for planning individual and group instruction, keeping families and other professionals informed of children's progress, and focusing future observations.

- **Portfolios with work samples**: Portfolios are collections of information and work samples that reflect children's progress toward the program outcomes. They can include important health information, a variety of work samples, checklists, photos, and other pertinent information that will help guide the teacher in documenting learning. Children are included in choosing which materials will go into the portfolios. These portfolios provide tangible evidence to the teacher and to families regarding individual strengths and needs. The material is examined every month by the teacher, with an eye toward adding new examples of positive growth.

INDIVIDUAL PROFILE

BASIC AND LITERACY OUTCOMES

Four- and Five-Year-Olds
Program Year 20__/20_

Reproduce a copy for each child.

Child's name: _____
Birth date: _____
Grade next year: _____
Assessor's name: _____

Enter dates to document the child's progress.

Outcomes*	Not Yet	Sometimes	Frequently	Almost Always
1. Knows first and last name (A)				
2. Writes first name and first letter of last name (L)				
3. Repeats home address (A)				
4. Knows purpose of and can dial 911 (A)				
5. Recognizes eleven basic colors (B)				
6. Counts from 1 to 31 (C)				
7. Recognizes numerals 1 to 10 out of order (D)				
8. Demonstrates an understanding of one-to-one correspondence				
9. Recites the alphabet				
10a. Identifies at least ten uppercase letters out of order (F)				
10b. Identifies at least ten lowercase letters out of order (G)				
11. Recognizes and names a square, circle, rectangle, and triangle (H)				
12. Copies a square, circle, rectangle, and triangle (I)				
13. Identifies basic body parts				
14. Reproduces basic body parts when drawing a person (M)				
15. Demonstrates appropriate cutting skills (N)				
16. Demonstrates appropriate pasting skills (O)				
17a. Understands the concept of print: Knows the difference between a letter, a word, and a sentence (P)				
17b. Understands the concept of print: Knows that print goes left to right and top to bottom with a return sweep (P)				
17c. Understands the concept of print: Knows that print tells the story and illustrations help tell the story (P)				
18a. Understands the concept of a story: Knows that an author writes the story (P)				
18b. Understands the concept of a story: Knows that an illustrator creates the pictures (P)				
18c. Understands the concept of a story: Knows that a story has a beginning, a middle, and an end				
18d. Understands the concept of a story: Knows there are different characters in a story				
18e. Understands the concept of a story: Knows the story has a setting where it takes place				
18f. Understands the concept of a story: Knows that a conversation might take place				
19. Predicts what comes next in a story (T)				
20. Retells a story with sufficient details (S)				
21. Differentiates and reproduces rhyming sounds (Q)				
22. Differentiates and reproduces beginning sounds (R)				
23. Shows growth in writing the alphabet and picture code systems				
24. Reads simple stories using pictures and/or words				
25. Shows growth in vocabulary and language use				
26. Identifies common words found inside and outside the classroom				
27. Understands and uses comparative terms				
28. Shows initiative in engaging in simple reading and writing activities				

Outcomes followed by letters in parentheses are measurable by the corresponding items on the Periodic Assessment Tool starting on page 18. Other outcomes should be assessed by other means, such as through observation and anecdotal recordings.

GROUP PROFILE
BASIC AND LITERACY OUTCOMES

Four- and Five-Year-Olds
Program Year 20___/20___

Shade in boxes as children show progress.

1 = Not Yet   3 = Frequently
2 = Sometimes   4 = Almost Always

Outcomes:

1. Knows first and last name (A)
2. Writes first name and first letter of last name (L)
3. Repeats home address (A)
4. Knows purpose of and can dial 911 (A)
5. Recognizes eleven basic colors (B)
6. Counts from 1 to 31 (C)
7. Recognizes numerals 1 to 10 out of order (D)
8. Demonstrates understanding of one-to-one correspondences
9. Recites the alphabet
10a. Identifies at least ten upper-case letters out of order (F)
10b. Identifies at least ten lower-case letters out of order (G)
11. Recognizes and names a square, circle, rectangle, and triangle (H)

Lessons for Literacy by Harlan S. Hansen and Ruth M. Hansen, copyright © 2010.

GROUP PROFILE
BASIC AND LITERACY OUTCOMES

Four- and Five-Year-Olds
Program Year 20__/20__

Shade in boxes as children show progress.

1 = Not Yet   3 = Frequently
2 = Sometimes   4 = Almost Always

Assessment items (each scored 1, 2, 3, 4):

- 12. Copies a square, circle, rectangle, and triangle (i)
- 13. Identifies basic body parts
- 14. Reproduces basic body parts when drawing a person (M)
- 15. Demonstrates appropriate cutting skills (N)
- 16. Demonstrates appropriate pasting skills (O)
- 17a. Understands the concept of print: Knows the difference between a letter, a word, and a sentence (P)
- 17b. Understands the concept of print: Knows that print goes left to right and top to bottom with a return sweep (P)
- 17c. Understands the concept of print: Knows that print tells the story and illustrations help tell the story (P)
- 18a. Understands the concept of a story: Knows that an author writes the story (P)
- 18b. Understands the concept of a story: Knows that an illustrator creates the pictures (P)
- 18c. Understands the concept of a story: Knows that a story has a beginning, a middle, and an end
- 18d. Understands the concept of a story: Knows there are different characters in a story

GROUP PROFILE
BASIC AND LITERACY OUTCOMES

Four- and Five-Year-Olds
Program Year 20___/20___

Shade in boxes as children show progress.

1 = Not Yet　　**3 = Frequently**
2 = Sometimes　**4 = Almost Always**

Column headings (each with a 1/2/3/4 scoring grid):

18e. Understands the concept of a story; knows where it takes place setting where it takes place

18f. Understands the concept of a story; Knows that a conversation might take place

19. Predicts what comes next in a story (T)

20. Retells a story with sufficient details (S)

21. Differentiates and reproduces rhyming sounds (Q)

22. Differentiates and reproduces beginning sounds (R)

23. Shows growth in writing the alphabet and picture code systems

24. Reads simple stories using pictures and/or words

25. Shows growth in vocabulary and language use

26. Identifies common words found inside and outside the classroom

27. Understands and uses comparative terms

28. Shows initiative in engaging in simple reading and writing activities

Periodic Assessment Tool

The following Periodic Assessment Tool was developed to help teachers identify the needs of each child in the classroom. From the results an individual program for each child can be developed that will meet individual needs. For example, if every child who enters the room in the fall can identify the color names, the teacher need not spend time teaching colors. On the other hand, if only a few children do not know the color names, small-group and individual instruction for those children is advised.

The assessment should be administered three times during the program year: fall (during the first month), winter, and spring. The results will provide an awareness of how the group of children is progressing in addition to how each individual child is progressing.

The assessment should be administered by the classroom teacher, director, or assistant teachers. It is not advised to have adult volunteers involved in this activity. The assessment will require approximately fifteen to twenty minutes per child. The test can be administered in one sitting or in segments over a few days, depending on the attention span of the child. You will need to duplicate the assessment for each child and have a pencil, crayons, scissors, and paste/glue available for the child's use. The person conducting the assessment will also need the proper color of ink pen to use as she keeps track of the child's responses. (The assessment form is designed so that the same form can be used in the fall, the winter, and the spring. Simply mark the form with a different color each time as specified in the instructions. This allows you to see progress from one assessment time to another.) If possible, find a quiet area in which to do the assessment.

The assessment information should be recorded for the corresponding outcomes on the Individual Profile and the Group Profile and used as you plan your daily instructional program. In the time between assessments, use anecdotal and observation information to record progress on various outcomes on the Individual Profile and the Group Profile.

Fall, Winter, and Spring Assessment

Reproduce a copy for each child.

Child's name _____

Birth date _____ Grade next year _____

Assessor's name_____

Dates of assessment: Fall _____ Winter _____ Spring_____

Marking: Fall = Red, Winter = Blue, Spring = Green

A. Personal information *underline correct responses*
Ask the child to provide the following information.

first name   last name   age   address   purpose of 911

B. Color recognition *underline correct responses*
Lay out the following colored crayons. Point to each crayon and have child name the color.

red   blue   green   yellow   orange   purple   brown

black   pink   grey   white

C. Counting *underline correct responses*
Arrange the crayons in a row. Have the child count the crayons by pointing to each one as they count.

1   2   3   4   5   6   7   8   9   10   11

D. Numeral recognition *see Numeral Recognition assessment form—underline correct responses*
Point to each numeral and ask the child to name it.

1   5   2   7   10   4   6   8   3   9   0

E. Auditory memory *underline correct responses*
Say each set of numbers and have the child repeat them in correct order.

5, 3   6, 4, 1   8, 3, 7, 1

F. Uppercase letter identification *see Uppercase Letter Identification assessment form*

Fall: number of letters correctly named _____

Winter: number of letters correctly named _____

Spring: number of letters correctly named _____

G. Lowercase letter identification *see Lowercase Letter Identification assessment form*

Fall: number of letters correctly named   _____

Winter: number of letters correctly named _____

Spring: number of letters correctly named _____

H. Shape recognition *see Shape Recognition and Copying assessment form—underline correct responses*

Point to each shape and ask the child to name it.

     circle   rectangle   square   triangle

I. Shape copying *see Shape Recognition and Copying assessment form—underline correct responses*

Ask the child to copy each shape in the space below it.

     circle   rectangle   square   triangle

Handedness *circle one:*   right   left   uncertain

Pencil/crayon grasp *underline response:* Holds firmly? Yes No   Holds correctly? Yes No

J. Pattern recreation

Set out a sequence of five blocks of different shapes and colors. Have a similar set on the table in random order. Ask the child to put the random blocks in the same order as the other set.

Fall: Yes _____ No _____

Winter: Yes _____ No _____

Spring: Yes _____ No _____

K. Reading *see Reading assessment form*

Fall: number of letters correctly identified   _____

Winter: number of letters correctly identified _____

Spring: number of letters correctly identified _____

L. Writes first name *see Writing assessment form—underline proficiency level*

     nothing   scribbles   some letters   full first name

M. Reproduces basic body parts *see Reproduces Basic Body Parts assessment form—underline proficiency level*

     Not yet   Developing   Proficient

N. Cutting skills *see Cutting and Pasting assessment form*

Handedness *circle one:*   right   left   uncertain

Scissors grasp

Fall: appropriate _____   needs development _____

Winter: appropriate _____   needs development _____

Spring: appropriate _____   needs development _____

Proficiency

Fall: poor _____   developing _____   skilled _____

Winter: poor _____   developing _____   skilled _____

Spring: poor _____   developing _____   skilled _____

O. Pasting skills *see Cutting and Pasting assessment form*

Fall: pastes on background paper _____   pastes on item to be pasted _____

Winter: pastes on background paper _____   pastes on item to be pasted _____

Spring: pastes on background paper _____   pastes on item to be pasted _____

Fall: uses too much paste _____   uses not enough paste _____   uses just enough paste _____

Winter: uses too much paste _____   uses not enough paste _____   uses just enough paste _____

Spring: uses too much paste _____   uses not enough paste _____   uses just enough paste _____

Additional Winter and Spring Assessment Items

P. Concepts of print *see Concepts of Print assessment form*

1. Identifies a separate letter: Yes ☐ No ☐
2. Identifies a separate word: Yes ☐ No ☐
3. Identifies a separate sentence: Yes ☐ No ☐
4. Points to where a sentence begins: Yes ☐ No ☐
5. Knows that print goes left to right: Yes ☐ No ☐
6. Knows that when a line ends there is a return sweep to the next line: Yes ☐ No ☐
7. Knows that an author writes the book: Yes ☐ No ☐
   Ask the child who writes a book.
8. Knows that an illustrator creates the pictures in a book: Yes ☐ No ☐
   Ask the child who creates the pictures in a book.

Q. Rhyming words *see Rhyming Words assessment form*

dig	Yes ☐ No ☐		got	Yes ☐ No ☐
fog	Yes ☐ No ☐		dark	Yes ☐ No ☐
rug	Yes ☐ No ☐		head	Yes ☐ No ☐
boy	Yes ☐ No ☐		bee	Yes ☐ No ☐

R. Beginning sounds *see Beginning Sounds assessment form*

sink	Yes ☐ No ☐		jump	Yes ☐ No ☐
red	Yes ☐ No ☐		give	Yes ☐ No ☐
more	Yes ☐ No ☐		lion	Yes ☐ No ☐
ball	Yes ☐ No ☐		toy	Yes ☐ No ☐

S. Retelling a story

Read the child the following story, and then ask the child to retell the story in her own words. Mark retelling as

Winter: not yet _____ developing ___ proficient _____
Spring: not yet _____ developing ___ proficient _____

One day a girl found a big red ball. She asked her brother to play with it. They went to the beach and tossed the ball back and forth. The ball went into the water. The kids called their mother to get the ball. It was wet and slippery. They had fun with the ball at the beach.

T. Predicts what comes next in a story

After retelling the above story, ask the child to tell you what he thinks happened afterward. Mark predicting as

Winter: not yet _____ developing ___ proficient _____
Spring: not yet _____ developing ___ proficient _____

Numeral Recognition: Fall, Winter, and Spring Assessment

Use with assessment item D.

Say to the child, "This year we are going to help you learn the numerals 0 to 10. You may not know them all now, but I want to find out which you already know so we can start from there."

1	5	2	7
10	4	6	8
3	9	0	

Uppercase Letter Identification: Fall, Winter, and Spring Assessment

Use with assessment item F.

Say to the child, "This year we are going to help you learn the letters in your first name. You may not know them all now, but I want to find out which ones you do know."

Fall assessment: Point only to the letters in the child's first name in random order and mark the child's correct responses (next to the corresponding letter) with a red marker. If the child knows all of the letters in his name, go to the top of the list of letters and continue until the child misses four in a row. Record the results on the Individual Profile and the Group Profile.

Winter assessment: Complete the procedure above using a blue marker. If the child knows all of the letters in her name, continue with the remaining list of letters.

Spring assessment: Complete the winter assessment using a green marker.

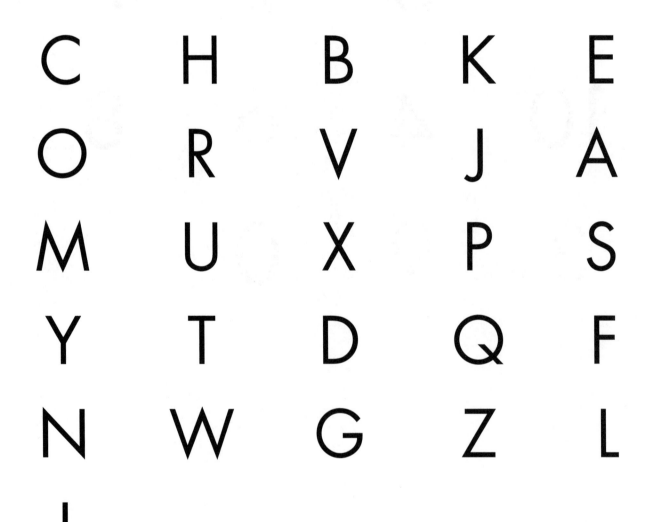

Lowercase Letter Identification: Fall, Winter, and Spring Assessment

Use with assessment item G.

Say to the child, "This year we are going to help you learn the letters in your first name. You may not know them all now, but I want to find out which ones you do know."

Fall assessment: Point only to the letters in the child's first name in random order and mark the child's correct responses (next to the corresponding letter) with a red marker. If the child knows all of the letters in her name, go to the top of the list of letters and continue until the child misses four in a row. Record the results on the Individual Profile and the Group Profile.

Winter assessment: Complete the procedure above using a blue marker. If the child doesn't know all of the letters in his name, continue on to the top of the page.

Spring assessment: Complete the winter assessment using a green marker.

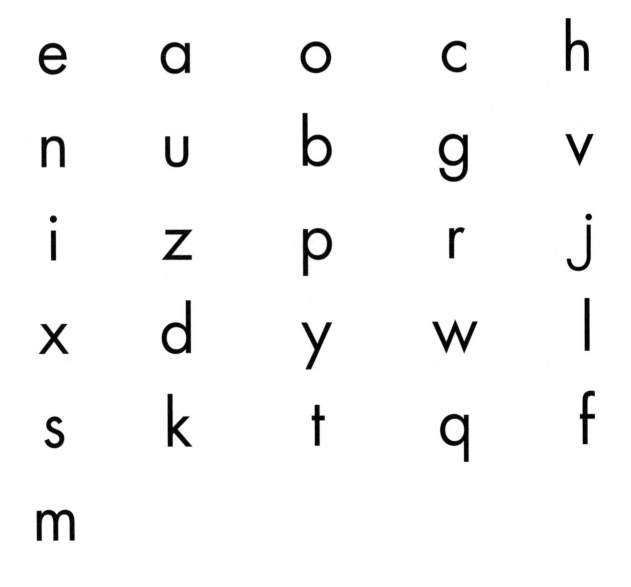

Shape Recognition and Copying: Fall Assessment

Use with assessment items H and I.

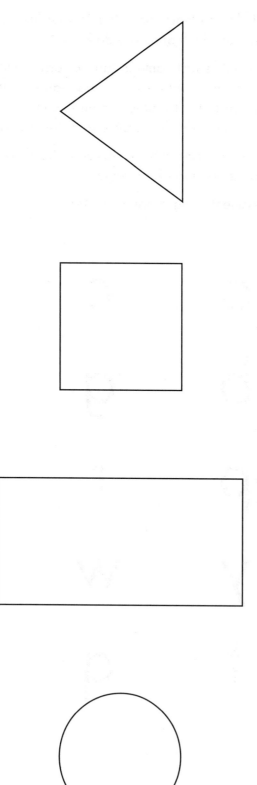

Point to these shapes one by one and ask each child to name them.

Ask the child to copy these shapes in the space below.

Shape Recognition and Copying: Winter Assessment

Use with assessment items H and I.

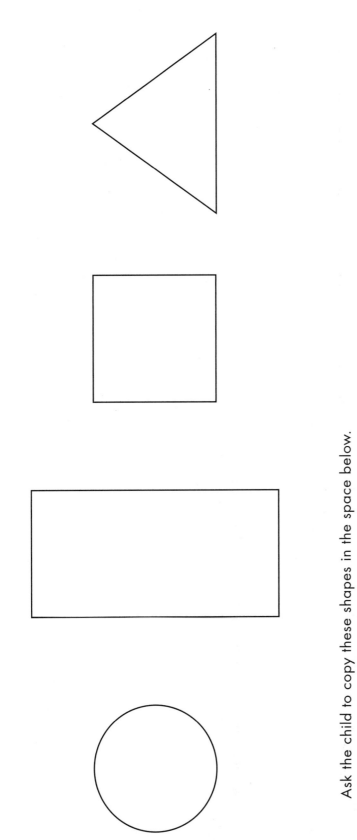

Point to these shapes one by one and ask each child to name them.

Ask the child to copy these shapes in the space below.

Shape Recognition and Copying: Spring Assessment

Use with assessment items H and I.

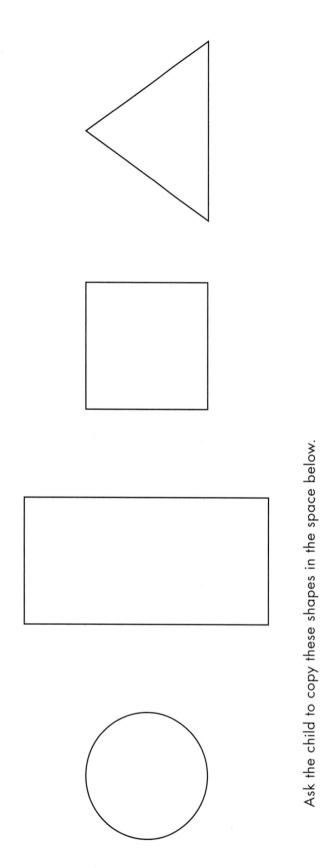

Point to these shapes one by one and ask each child to name them.

Ask the child to copy these shapes in the space below.

Reading: Fall, Winter, and Spring Assessment

Use with assessment item K.

Ask the child if she can read the following sentences. Assure the child that most children cannot yet read but that they will be learning about reading during the year. Stop when it is obvious that the child is unable to complete the task. The purpose of this activity is to identify the early reader or those who know some words by sight.

Fall: Underline correct responses in red.

Winter: Underline correct responses in blue.

Spring: Underline correct responses in green.

See the cat.

Look at me.

I am big.

The dog can run fast.

Writing: Fall Assessment

Use with assessment item L.

Ask the child to write his or her first name and first letter of last name below.

Writing: Winter Assessment

Use with assessment item L.

Ask the child to write her or his first name and first letter of last name below.

Writing: Spring Assessment

Use with assessment item L.

Ask the child to write his or her first name and first letter of last name below.

Reproduces Basic Body Parts: Fall Assessment

Use with assessment item M.

Ask the children to draw a picture of a person below. Provide no assistance. The purpose is to see what experience each child brings to the program. Mark each child's proficiency on the assessment sheet.

Reproduces Basic Body Parts: Winter Assessment

Use with assessment item M.

Ask the children to draw a picture of a person below. Provide no assistance. Mark each child's proficiency on the assessment sheet.

Reproduces Basic Body Parts: Spring Assessment

Use with assessment item M.

Ask the children to draw a picture of a person below. Provide no assistance. Mark each child's proficiency on the assessment sheet.

Cutting and Pasting: Fall Assessment

Use with assessment items N and O.

For this item, use the reproducible tree outlines provided after the spring Cutting and Pasting assessment page. Ask the children to cut out the tree and paste it below. Provide no assistance. Record each child's basic ability to cut and paste on the assessment sheet. This can be done in a small-group setting to save time.

Cutting and Pasting: Winter Assessment

Use with assessment items N and O.

For this item, use the reproducible tree outlines provided after the spring Cutting and Pasting assessment page. Ask the children to cut out the tree and paste it below. Provide no assistance. Record each child's basic ability to cut and paste on the assessment sheet. This can be done in a small-group setting to save time.

Cutting and Pasting: Spring Assessment

Use with assessment items N and O.

For this item, use the reproducible tree outlines provided after the spring Cutting and Pasting assessment page. Ask the children to cut out the tree and paste it below. Provide no assistance. Record each child's basic ability to cut and paste on the assessment sheet. This can be done in a small-group setting to save time.

Concepts of Print: Winter and Spring Assessment

Use with assessment item P.

Ask the following questions. Indicate whether or not the child can complete the task.

"Show me which of these is a letter standing all by itself—just one letter."

Yes ☐ **No** ☐

"Show me which of these is a word standing all by itself—just one word."

Yes ☐ **No** ☐

"Show me which of these is a sentence."

Yes ☐ **No** ☐

"Show me, by pointing with your finger, where I would start reading these sentences."

Yes ☐ **No** ☐

If child stops at end of line, say "Where would I go next? Show me."

Yes ☐ **No** ☐

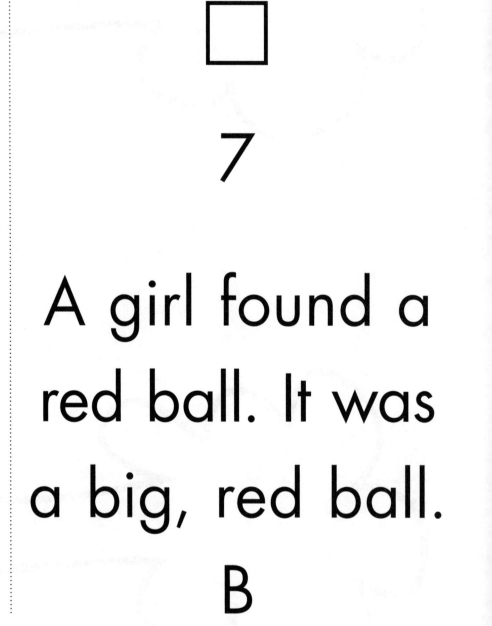

Cat

☐

7

A girl found a red ball. It was a big, red ball.

B

Rhyming Words: Winter and Spring Assessment

Use with assessment item Q.

This assessment assumes that the children have been introduced to rhyming words during the fall months.

Say to the child, "I'm going to say a word and I want you to give me a word that rhymes with my word. For example, *bill* and *mill*. Now tell me a word that rhymes with *bat*." Use other examples for practice, such as *fan* (*ran, tan*) and *sit* (*fit, hit*).

Ask the child to tell you a word that rhymes with each of the words listed below. Accept nonsense words. Mark yes or no on assessment item Q.

1. dig
2. got
3. fog
4. dark
5. rug
6. head
7. boy
8. bee

Discontinue assessment if child misses three consecutive words.

Beginning Sounds: Winter and Spring Assessment

Use with assessment item R.

Say to the child, "Words can begin with the same sound—like the words *ball* and *baby*. They both begin with the *b* sound. Tell me a word that begins with the same sound as *pie* (*party, peanut*). Tell me a word that begins with the same sound as *fast* (*friend, fun*)."

Ask the child to tell you a word that begins with the same sound as each of the words listed below. Mark yes or no on assessment item R.

1. sink
2. jump
3. red
4. give
5. more
6. lion
7. ball
8. toy

Discontinue assessment if child misses three consecutive words.

Child Adjustment to Environment Inventory: Fall, Winter, and Spring Assessment

Child's name _____

Birth date _____Grade next year_____

Assessor's name_____

Please place an X on the mark that best describes the child. Add marks in the winter and spring (with blue and green ink, respectively) to show changes.

Perfectionist—frustrates easily if something is not perfect	├──┼──┼──┤	Can accept and learn from mistakes
Moves easily from one activity to the next	├──┼──┼──┤	Has great difficulty changing activities
Needs an environment with only one activity going on	├──┼──┼──┤	Works well in an environment with many things going on at once
Needs quiet surroundings to concentrate	├──┼──┼──┤	Able to concentrate with significant noise
Needs consistent routine	├──┼──┼──┤	Goes with the flow, is comfortable with changes in plans
Is able to focus even with lots going on around	├──┼──┼──┤	Is easily distracted
Needs to work individually	├──┼──┼──┤	Works well in groups
Makes friends easily	├──┼──┼──┤	Has a hard time making friends
Self-motivated	├──┼──┼──┤	Does the bare minimum
Excited learner	├──┼──┼──┤	Needs encouragement
Firstborn	├──┼──┼──┤	Fifth child

Oral Language Checklist: Periodic Assessment

Child's name _____

Birth date _____ Grade next year_____

Assessor's name_____

Every month or so, obseve the child and record his oral language development.

Key: N = Not at this time   S = Sometimes   M = Most of the time

DATE										

SPEECH SKILLS

Uses appropriate volume										
Articulates clearly										

SETTINGS

Talks to teachers										
Talks to peers										
Talks in small-group situations										
Talks in large-group situations										

LANGUAGE USE

Asks for help from peers										
Asks for help from adults										
Asks questions										
Initiates conversations										
Takes turns speaking										
Relates personal experiences										
Responds relevantly to topics										
Expresses point of view										
Expresses feelings										
Retells a sequence of events from experience										

Writing Anecdotal Reports

Anecdotal reports are brief, informal, dated descriptions of a child's development. They are a powerful tool for collecting information at regular intervals. Anecdotal reports can be used to document social, physical, emotional, and intellectual development; however, the focus in this book is on how anecdotal reports can be used to show a child's growth in basic and literacy skills.

Keeping anecdotal records can enhance a teacher's classroom observation skills. Memory alone does not sufficiently capture all aspects of a child's progress over the year. By systematically recording brief descriptions of a child's growth, teachers are able to make better decisions about how to meet a child's learning needs.

Anecdotal reports can be used for planning instruction, documenting and keeping others informed of a child's progress, and focusing future observations. As mentioned earlier, the purpose of assessment is to provide information on how to direct a child's learning. Assessments provide information that can be shared with other caregivers in the program, with professionals called in to deal with special situations, with teachers of programs into which a child will progress, and with families. The more practice you have observing and recording a child's progress, the greater is the probability that you will be able to plan experiences that enhance learning.

Anecdotal reports focus on an individual child. These observations can be made during many parts of the day when children are involved in natural settings. You can observe what a child is doing, or you can intercede with a request that involves the child for a short period of time. For example, while observing a child in the library corner, you might ask the child to show you, in the book she is practicing reading, the direction in which print moves on the page.

Anecdotal reports can also include a small group of children who are working together on a project. On a separate recording sheet you can include information on several or all of the children in the group.

What to Include and What Not to Include

When writing anecdotal reports, be mindful of the following suggestions that will make the observations as meaningful as possible:

- Document the date and time of day the observation takes place. Also include the name of the person making the observation.

- Record the facts. These include
  - the activity in which the child is involved;
  - a description of the child's surroundings;
  - how the child responds to his environment;
  - details of the child's actions and interactions.
- Write down exactly what the child is doing and/or saying—*not* what you think is happening. Observations must be objective, unbiased, and accurate.
- Avoid labels, intentions, evaluations, judgments, and negatives.
- Avoid drawing conclusions about the child while you are conducting the observation. No opinions or judgments should ever be made in an anecdotal report. Judgments can be made by comparing a series of observations, not when documenting just one.

A Useful Technique

There are different techniques for observing and recording a child's learning. Here is one efficient method. You will need a clipboard, sheets of computer labels, and a three-ring binder with paper. Write each child's name on an individual sheet of paper and place it in the binder. Have additional sheets of paper available as needed for individual children and for students who enter throughout the year. Clip the computer labels onto the clipboard, and write your observations on the labels.

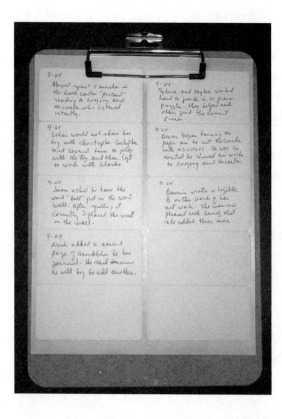

Keep the computer labels on the clipboard. At the end of each day, peel off the labels on which you have written and place them on each child's page in the binder. This will provide you with an easy way to store your ongoing records of individual progress, strengths, weaknesses, and needs throughout the year. Transfer appropriate information to the Individual Profile and Group Profile as needed.

Schedule of Reporting

There are two important things to remember as you plan to make anecdotal reporting part of your classroom life. First, you need to allow adequate time for observation and recording. Children should not be rushed. Second, you need to observe and record a child's behavior on a regular basis over time. Making a weekly commitment is a good way to set a schedule.

For each week, identify one or two of the program outcomes and observe each child during that week. For example, the outcome might be growth in recognizing or writing their names. Later in the year, outcomes might focus on predicting and retelling stories. Setting weekly goals provides a systematic opportunity to complete regular observations. Focus your comments on the chosen outcomes.

During some weeks, you might choose to focus on the children instead of the outcomes. Observe them in the settings in which you find them. Focus your comments on whatever happens during that time, not just on program outcomes.

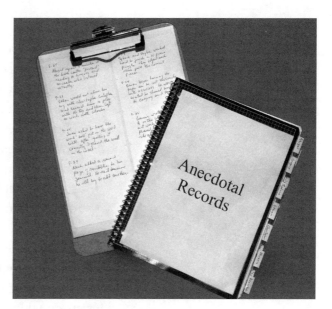

Portfolios

A portfolio is a powerful tool for developing a comprehensive profile of each child. It is based on a selected collection of each child's work, with pieces chosen to reflect the program's learning goals, the broad range of activities in the classroom, and evidence of the child's efforts, achievements, and progress in learning. The items should be collected regularly as part of children's daily work, and each entry should be dated. As you build a portfolio, include

- items required of all children;
- items unique to each child;
- items that reflect the entire curriculum.

Here are some tips for setting up a portfolio system in your classroom:
- At the beginning of each year, prepare a folder for each child and designate a convenient place to store them.
- Discuss with the children the purpose of the portfolio. Talk about some of the items they will be adding throughout the year.
- Regularly add new information and examples to every portfolio. Items you can place in the children's folders include

  - individual progress forms updated on a regular basis (at least monthly);
  - fall, winter, and spring assessment forms;
  - samples of artwork, social studies and science projects, examples of cutting and pasting, writing samples, evidence of literacy development, and so on;

- anecdotal reports;
- health information, such as height, weight, medication schedule (where appropriate), record of required immunizations, and any recorded daily health problems;
- photos taken at the beginning and the end of the year and photos taken during the year in various classroom activities;
- language samples captured on audiotape;
- specific checklists;
- other pertinent information.

- Announce to the children ahead of time that their work on a particular day will be added to their portfolios so they will not be disappointed that they can't take their work home. If a child insists on taking work home, make a photocopy for the portfolio.
- Periodically review the files to determine what is important to keep and what can be given back to the children and families.
- Use the information from the portfolio to

- individualize the curriculum for each child;
- update the Individual Profile and the Group Profile;
- conduct a family-teacher conference;
- meet with a medical or other specialist.

Note: Be selective. Do not let portfolios become catchalls for every bit of work completed by a child. Keep older items only when they can be contrasted with a more recent similar piece to show progress.

A Note about Three-Year-Olds

The preschool years are commonly thought of as ages three to five. However, manipulative and cognitive abilities vary widely between the third and fourth years of life as well as between the fourth and fifth years. This does not mean that three-year-olds cannot be in programs with older children, but appropriate expectations for three-year-olds should be kept in mind. On the page that follows, we have provided an Individual Profile specifically for three-year-olds involved in this program. The outcomes suggested should be observed, not formally assessed.

The emphasis on assessment and instruction rightly begins with four-year-olds. A three-year-old's experiences are about exposure more than attempts to produce and assess the outcomes expected from older children. As three-year-olds participate in classroom experiences, they gain a foundation for the next year. Teachers should never alter discussions because three-year-olds are present. Younger children understand communication before they can verbalize responses and will learn more than they are able to acknowledge. In other words, the learning stays with them. In another year, when their vocabulary catches up with their knowledge, teachers can involve the children in the complete assessment and outcome activities suggested in this book.

INDIVIDUAL PROFILE
BASIC AND LITERACY OUTCOMES

Three-Year-Olds
Program Year 20___/20_

Enter dates to document the child's progress.

Child's name: _____

Birth date: _____

Grade next year: _____

Assessor's name: _____

Outcomes	Not Yet	Sometimes	Frequently	Almost Always
1. Knows first name				
2. Identifies first letter in name				
3. Makes beginning attempts to write first name				
4. Knows primary colors (red, blue, yellow)				
5. Counts from 1 to his or her age				
6. Recognizes and names a square and a circle				
7. Can identify basic body parts (head, chest, belly, arms, legs, fingers, toes)				
8. Demonstrates beginning cutting skills				
9. Demonstrates beginning pasting skills				
10. Understands the concept of print: Can point to the direction of print as left to right				
11. Begins to identify rhyming sounds				
12. Shows growth in vocabulary and language use				
13. Uses words to communicate needs to an adult				

PART TWO

Classroom
Essentials

2

Classroom Essentials

Successful early childhood programs reflect certain indispensable elements. These elements range from specific teaching activities to the overall organization of the educational environment. We refer to these as *classroom essentials.*

Two Foundations

Underlying the classroom essentials are two important foundations upon which the success of the curriculum program rests. The essentials serve as the overarching framework that holds the program together and guarantees an ever-evolving partnership between the important adults involved in children's education.

The first foundation is a dedicated and caring staff. The success of any program depends on the staff working together for the benefit of all children. This goal is accomplished when the following characteristics are observed among the staff:

- The entire team—director, teachers, assistant teachers, health personnel, nutrition workers—shares the same goals and reinforces them in their respective roles.
- They support each other during trying times.
- They are helpful and kind to children in their care.
- They seek out avenues for professional growth, and they share those ideas among themselves.
- They respect the individuality of families.
- They truly enjoy their jobs as caregivers.

The second foundation is a positive home-school partnership. Families want assurance that their children's teachers know what they are doing and care about the children in their program. It is the responsibility of the program to provide this assurance. *Lessons for Literacy* is a tool to help you provide that assurance because it is a curriculum program with defined outcomes. The results of the outcomes provide evidence that demonstrates children's growth and how the program is serving the children in it:

- Individual assessments show each child's progress and are routinely updated.
- Anecdotal reports pinpoint specific growth and needs.
- Examples of each child's work are collected in individual portfolios.
- Letters to families explain upcoming curriculum events and suggest ways for families to follow up at home.
- Scheduled and unscheduled family-teacher conferences are encouraged.
- Classroom visits enable family members to see the program in operation.
- Adult family members are given the opportunity to be resource persons in the classroom.

It is the sum of all the planned contacts between the home and the school that provides families with the assurance that teachers know what they are doing and care for each child.

Twenty-One Classroom Essentials

Once the foundations are in place, individual teachers can focus on providing the classroom essentials. We have identified twenty-one classroom essentials for consideration in preschool programs:

1. Effective Calendars
2. An I'll Wait Timeline
3. News Bulletin Boards
4. Teacher Photos
5. Individual Attendance Devices
6. Super Star of the Week
7. Data-Collecting Activities

8. Language Experience Stories
9. Yearlong Birthday Calendar
10. Helpers Charts
11. Words in the Environment
12. Song Charts
13. Alphabet and Number Charts
14. Literacy Centers
15. Labeled Bulletin Boards
16. Writing Materials
17. Word Walls
18. Maps
19. Comfortable Group Meeting Areas
20. Classroom Centers
21. Field Trips and Resource People

The following pages provide a general description, an explanation, and a rationale for each classroom essential. In addition, there are specific guidelines for setting up and using each one.

Effective Calendars

Calendars, and also the lack of calendars, in early childhood programs represent certain beliefs in teaching and learning. For example, some programs have banned calendars, fearing that teachers will focus on children's rote memorization of days, weeks, months, and numbers. In other preschool centers, calendars are nonexistent because they are deemed too complicated for young children. On the other end of the spectrum, an increasing number of centers now use a kindergarten version of a calendar to teach numbers and certain terms—*year, month, day, today, yesterday, tomorrow,* and so on. Teachers start with day one and add a new number each day.

The problem with this method is that it does not deal with events, like upcoming birthdays, until those dates are reached. This type of calendar functions more as a number game than it does as a calendar. An effective calendar stimulates number knowledge and focuses on functional counting. It also fosters language development by expanding language opportunities.

Here's How
Provide a three-inch square for each day so the calendar measures at least twenty-one inches (to include seven days) by fifteen inches (to include five weeks). This will allow ample room to include details about

important and interesting information that is happening on any given day. (Include the actual date in an upper left corner, not using too much space.) Put birthday cakes with a child's name and photo on the appropriate dates. Include birthdays of staff members so children can be a part of their birthday celebrations too. Add a picture of a van or bus for field trips. Highlight any program observances such as family-teacher conferences and open houses. Note days the program will be closed for holidays, teacher in-service days, and so on. Jot down the names of any resource people who will be visiting. Put in age-appropriate highlights about world, national, and community observances you think might be of interest to the children: Scarecrow Day, National Neighborhood Day, World Gratitude Day, and the birthdays of famous artists, musicians, and world leaders. Use a stick pin or other marker to identify the current date, and use the calendar to count forward to upcoming events and backward to past events. This allows children repetition in counting, but is purposeful in doing so.

OCTOBER 2009

Sunday	Monday	Tuesday	Wednesday	Thursday	Friday	Saturday
				1 National Popcorn Month	2	3
4	5	6 Open House	7	8	9	10
11	12 Columbus Day	13	14	15	16 Anna	17
18	19	20 Field Trip	21	22	23	24
25	26 Danny	27	28	29	30	31 Halloween

An I'll Wait Timeline

Who hasn't heard excited children asking over and over about upcoming special events? The refrain goes something like this: "How long before . . . ?" An I'll Wait Timeline allows children to keep track of the remaining time while also helping them learn to count backward.

Here's How

This photo shows a good example of a reverse number line. It sets up anticipation for an upcoming event and helps children to learn to count backward. It has a sliding arrow to move each day, and a different symbol can be used to show the upcoming event: a van or bus for a field trip, a person for a guest, a party symbol to match the special occasion, and so on. An example with some basic elements of an I'll Wait Timeline appears in the appendix.

News Bulletin Boards

The classroom environment should reflect the out-of-school environment through bulletin boards and discussions. Newspapers and magazines are full of stories that highlight important, humorous, and unique city, state, and national events. Children are often vaguely aware of these stories from family discussions at home or through media exposure. The news might be about a new animal at the zoo, a fire that destroyed a house where young children were heroically saved, or a truck that overturned on the highway. While children's understanding of displayed stories might not be too deep, the teacher's discussion with the class can bring the news to the children's level.

Here's How

Set aside a space for your news bulletin board. For children this age, the teacher can bring in the majority of items to display. Over the course of the year, children may be motivated to add items. However, remember that many homes do not receive a newspaper, or if they do, they may not involve children in discussions about the stories. The newspaper is a great source of information, and for young children, it is a wonderful source of language development and problem-solving opportunities when teachers help them interact with the material.

Teacher Photos

Children and families are excited about meeting and getting to know their teachers. Taking home a photo of the teacher or teachers helps solidify that relationship. The special twist suggested for these photos below gives an early indication of what children know about body parts and how well they can draw them.

Here's How

At the beginning of the year, place the photo faces of classroom teachers on a sheet of paper, leaving sufficient room for children to draw in body parts. Have each teacher sign the bottom of the page under each face. Have the children, with no adult assistance, complete the bodies and put whatever mark or writing they wish to have represent their own names. Allow the children to take the sheets home to put in their own special place.

There will be a vast difference in manipulative abilities and knowledge among the children. Accept each child's drawing with equal enthusiasm. You can determine who knows how to write their name, who knows only the first initial of their name, who scribbles, and to what extent children are aware of and can reproduce body parts. Mark these levels on the assessment sheet.

Individual Attendance Devices

Teaching children to take responsibility is an ongoing goal of educational programs. One way to help children work on this goal is to have them check in each day. This lets teachers know who is present. Some children assume this responsibility immediately while others need regular encouragement until it becomes a daily practice. In the process, children reinforce their counting skills by noting how many are "here" and how many are "not here." Using attendance devices also builds the concept of one-to-one correspondence.

Here's How

During the first week of the fall program, have children make individual check-in devices. This will allow you to have an independent roll-call system. The actual devices can be varied throughout the year.

Pictured to the left are a name-stick system and a name-strip system. For the stick system, have the children draw their faces and cut out the drawings—or use small photos. Attach each child's drawing or photo to a piece of construction paper with the child's name written on it. Then attach the paper to a tongue depressor. As the children arrive at the program every day, have them find their name sticks and place them in the "here" container. In a few months, take off the pictures and let them select by name only. The name slips work the same way.

Super Star of the Week

Many preschool programs highlight a child of the week, often with a bulletin board to which families can contribute photos and personal items. One of the problems with this method is that it depends on family participation. Some weeks the bulletin board might be full of items, but during another week it could be almost bare. This is not fair to children whose families do not or cannot provide the needed materials. Activities in the classroom need to be fair for everyone.

Here's How

This system of highlighting students ensures that each child is recognized equally. Attach several pieces of paper together to form a simple list of preferences or characteristics that each child can provide when asked, for example, a favorite food, favorite color, favorite movie, favorite television program, or favorite ice-cream flavor. You can add other personal information such as "I am happy when _____." and "My favorite place to go is _____." This list is only limited by your ideas. Once the list is compiled, laminate the pages and attach them to a bulletin board. To highlight a child, start by putting up the child's photo. Then, in a class discussion, feature the child chosen as the Super Star and have him or her respond to the questions as you write the answers in the appropriate spaces.

Data-Collecting Activities

Learning about ourselves and others is always an enjoyable and worthwhile activity. Quantifying and coming to conclusions about the information adds an important dimension. A permanent grid chart provides many opportunities to count, to compare, and to contrast children's interests and personal traits.

Here's How

Create a permanent grid chart to use in data-collecting activities. On a piece of light construction paper, construct a grid of at least one hundred squares. Laminate the grid. Once a week conduct a simple data-collecting activity by asking questions such as, "How many brothers and sisters are in your family?" "What color hair (or eyes) do you have?" and "What is your favorite food?" There is no end to the various kinds of information to explore! Initially, write in children's names so they can see their preferences. As they understand graphing, a simple X will suffice. This activity provides opportunities for children to think of their responses, to see where their preferences fit within the group's preferences, and to practice counting the results. It also allows for experiences with comparative terms, such as *more than*, *less than*, and *same as*.

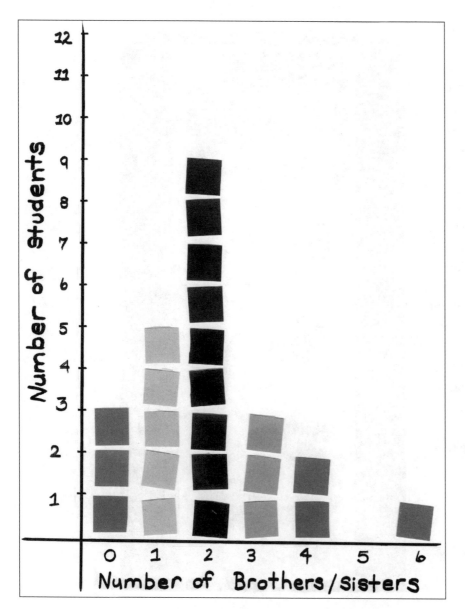

Language Experience Stories

Language experience stories can be generated by the teacher or the children. They can be related to some topic under study or a field trip, or they can be used to explore knowledge and feelings. The teacher asks the questions and writes down the children's responses. Together they review the responses, look for similar letters in words, look for capitalization and punctuation marks, and read the story. Making these stories available to children after the activity is over allows individual children to revisit the story and for the teacher to refer to the story when giving individual help.

Here's How

This illustration shows an actual language experience story. The children visited an apple orchard as a class, and then shared their story ideas with the teacher, who wrote them down in sentences (which explains the inappropriate grammar). They then decided to identify and count all of the *a*'s in the story. Another day they might look for *n*'s or *o*'s and so on.

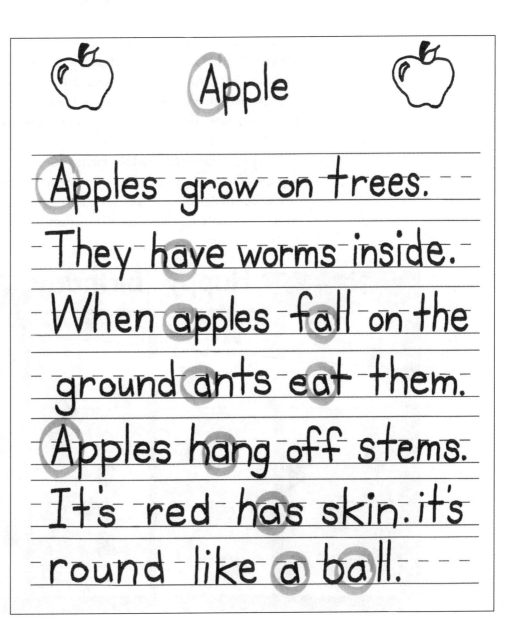

Apple

Apples grow on trees.
They have worms inside.
When apples fall on the
ground ants eat them.
Apples hang off stems.
It's red has skin. it's
round like a ball.

Yearlong Birthday Calendar

Current classroom practices for tracking birthdays have little relationship to the actual event. A birthday train on a bulletin board or candy canes in a candy jar ignore the fact that a birthday is a specific day in a specific month. The yearlong birthday calendar recognizes this fact and also highlights those birthdays that occur when children are not in school.

Here's How

There are two alternatives for creating a yearlong birthday chart: (1) Construct or purchase a twelve-month calendar grid and laminate it so it can be used over and over. Each year, write out the new dates on the calendar grid, adding small photos of children on their birthdates. This reminds children that birthdays are dates on the calendar. Summer birthdays are easily identifiable and can be celebrated at half birthdays or in the month preceding the end of the spring session. (2) Every year, purchase a large full-year calendar and put photos of the children on their birthdays.

As you discuss the yearlong birthday chart with the children, make a graph of how many birthdays there are in each month. Use comparative words to demonstrate the varied use of the information. This type of activity combines the value of a yearlong birthday chart and a data-collecting activity.

Helpers Charts

One good way to help children learn to take responsibility is to use them as classroom helpers who perform assigned classroom jobs. A system that helps children look ahead to identify the tasks and their days for helping creates anticipation and fosters name recognition. A simple photo calendar that shows the current day works well.

Here's How

Some teachers have found it useful to have one or two helpers a day rather than a single child having a task every day or five children having tasks over a week. This gives children many jobs to do on their day, building greater responsibility for different areas of the room. A photo calendar, like the one shown below that shows the current day, helps remind children when their time is approaching. They can even count the number of days until they are the designated helper. As the year goes by, the pictures can be changed to names.

Words in the Environment

We need to encourage children to begin reading simple environmental print—signs and words that they see in the classroom, around the school building, and elsewhere in their immediate surroundings. Words commonly seen in the environment include *stop, go, push, pull, in,* and *out,* as well as popular brand names. In many cases, children will identify the colors, logos, and sign shapes they recognize and then read them. Through regular exposure, children can begin to read the "word code," and from there, transfer what they're seeing to the "alphabet code."

Here's How

Collect pictures, photos, and other sources of words commonly found in the environment and then choose those that have a picture or visual clue identified with them. These clues can include sign shapes (triangles, circles, and so on). Have the children try to recognize the words by linking them to the pictures or visual clues. From there, you can expand the activit to help children recognize common words, such as *in* or *out* on a store door.

Song Charts

Children enjoy listening to music and singing songs. Music time should be included as a scheduled activity in all programs. Music is also a very effective tool for facilitating transitions from one activity to another. Children can learn tunes easily, but they have trouble remembering all the lyrics. A set of charts for familiar song lyrics helps children remember the words, increases word and numeral recognition, and enables them to sing the songs.

Here's How
Construct song charts with both words and pictures. (See an example on page 83.) Words and pictures allow all children to be successful in reading the words to the song. From time to time, cover the picture so children can focus on the words. Cover and uncover the pictures during the year to make sure all the children feel comfortable. By the end of the year, children will know songs both from memory and from recognition of the words.

Alphabet and Number Charts

Alphabet and number charts provide reference points for teachers to use in working with groups or individual children during activities that include the alphabet and numbers.

Here's How
Commercial alphabet and number charts are readily available at teacher and office supply stores. Hung on preschool classroom walls, these charts are excellent resources for natural, teachable moments with children. They should not be used, however, for rote skill instruction.

Literacy Centers

The mere existence of a literary center highlights the importance of books within the program. The literary center should include an assortment of books on a variety of topics. It should also offer a variety of media (a tape player, a CD or MP3 player, and a DVD player). This variety allows children to develop their interest in books through many outlets. Put a picture dictionary and encyclopedia in the center for children to explore and demonstrate their use when questions arise or during the study of a topic.

Here's How

An inviting literacy center filled with a variety of resources for children is important for every preschool classroom to have. What makes a center inviting? Providing comfortable places to sit, making sure children can easily reach everything, and turning books with their covers facing out are some ways to draw children in. Remember to include a picture dictionary and a children's encyclopedia in the center for children to explore. Demonstrate how to use these resources when a question arises or during the study of a topic.

Labeled Bulletin Boards

Every preschool center has children involved in projects. These projects might be creating artwork or they could be a unit project. Very often the results of the projects end up on bulletin boards. Label the projects posted on the bulletin boards so children learn that words describe the activity in which they were involved. This adds to their continued involvement in learning the role of print and in the decoding process.

Here's How

One instructive first bulletin-board project to do with children is self-portraits. Prior to conducting the winter assessment of the children's ability to draw a body, initiate a discussion about how each child is alike and different in appearance. Talk about height, eye color, length and color of hair, dimples, skin color, freckles, and other traits. Show the children pictures of self-portraits painted by well-known artists. Have the children discuss the portraits in terms of eye color, skin color, hair color, and clothing

Show the children how they will paint themselves. Standing in front of the classroom, have the children identify your features—hair color, eye color, face shape, and so on. On a piece of easel paper, model the process by completing a simple self-portrait as the children observe.

For the children, place a mirror near the easels, then select several children to begin their self-portraits, while the other children are involved in choice time. This provides opportunities for the teacher to work with a few individual children as they examine their unique characteristics in preparation for their painting. Select several more children each day until they are all finished. Completing this activity in choice time over the week allows sufficient time for the teacher to help each child with her drawing, pointing out unique features. It also allows children who need more time to complete their drawings to do so, even completing a redo if necessary. Finally, this method provides an opportunity for teachers to assess which children need more instruction. Display the completed self-portraits on a bulletin board for follow-up discussion, and then send the portraits home as a special gift for their families.

Writing Materials

Rooms should be equipped with a wide variety of writing materials besides the usual crayons and pencils. Providing pens, markers, paintbrushes, and chalk gives the children many different sensory experiences and helps them learn that different writing devices produce different results in size, shape, and color.

Here's How

Remember to broaden the range of writing instruments, paper, and other surfaces on which to write. Writing can be done outdoors, using chalk, paintbrushes dipped in water, or sticks in sand. Small chalkboards, self-stick notes, index cards, and scratch pads are inexpensive items on which children can write with different media.

Word Walls

The purpose of a classroom word wall is to provide a well-organized, consistent, and visible place for children to reference when copying new and familiar words into their writing. The word wall should contain a matrix of the alphabet and some words that start with each letter. Over time, the word wall becomes a valuable reference for both the children and the teacher.

Here's How

The word wall is an important resource for children as they develop writing skills through journaling and other writing activities. Many teachers begin a word wall with the first names of all the children in the class. A digital camera makes it easy to post the children's pictures with their names. As the children write and ask for the spelling of certain

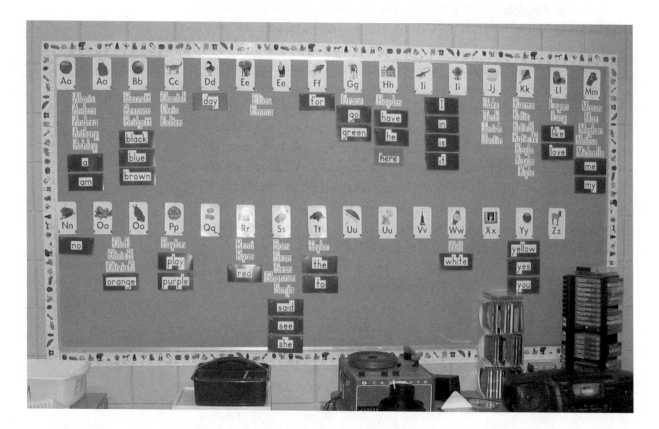

words, add those words to the word wall. If possible, include a picture with the word, which provides additional support for understanding new words. When children are involved in writing activities, such as journaling, it is important for you to help them use the word wall as a reference for familiar words.

If you know the reading program for the kindergarten level, find out the sight words that are used in the program and add those words to the wall when children need to use them in their writing.

Maps

Have area, city and town, state, national, and world maps to use when occasions arise. The purpose here is not to help children learn map skills, but to let children know there are sources to go to in order to acquire information.

Here's How
Maps are viewed as helpful tools by preschool children when the maps are directly relevant to their experiences. For example, if a child mentions that his grandmother is coming from another state, help the children find that state (and city) on a map. Maps are also excellent supplemental resources for news-based discussions. When critical events happen, such as floods, fires, and other disasters, locate these areas and talk about what is happening to the people and how they are coping.

Comfortable Group Meeting Areas

The vast majority of textbooks in early childhood education use the term circle time to describe parts of the program where children meet as a group. Circle time, however, may not be the most effective way to organize children's seating on all occasions. For example, circle time is very useful when having an open discussion with children, because they are communicating directly with one another. This eye contact is especially important when dealing with interpersonal relationship problems, such as how to treat each other. Yet, when reading a story, circle time causes some problems with sight lines. Some children who are facing the same way as the teachers cannot see and try to move out into the circle and turn around to face the book.

Similarly, insisting that children stay on a letter taped to the floor or on their own piece of carpet creates situations when children cannot see or hear what's going on. It is better for all children to face the teacher when reading a book, when discussing the calendar and the weather, when dealing with a theme discussion, and when doing a language experience story.

Here's How

Using a corner in the classroom provides natural boundaries for children to sit and interact with the teacher and with each other during group time. Children should not be asked to sit in a specific spot or with a certain posture. For example, the order to "criss-cross applesauce" presents a less than personal manner for settling children and puts them in a less than comfortable position.

Classroom Centers

Every early childhood teacher has been trained in the use of class-room centers and knows that centers should be filled with appropriate materials for all interests and ability levels. Yet, visits to a variety of classrooms across the country attest to the actual extent that training is implemented in the classroom. In one state where the classroom ratio of four-year-old children to teachers is twenty to one, there is little room for centers after providing tables for all the children, an area to convene for group activities, and a storage area for cots or sleeping bags. In other places, there are few centers because of the cost of equipping them. In some instances, few centers are set up because teachers have a minimum amount of training and don't understand the concept or find it to be too much work.

The ways in which children interact with centers is also an issue. When the schedule says "choice time" or "free time," how free is that choice? When children are assigned to centers where the number of children has no relationship to the activity, it changes the intent of this block of time. Often problems occur because children are bored in a center not of their choosing and want to go somewhere else in the room. The majority of successful programs have centers that reflect children's interests (art, games and puzzles, nature, physical fitness, literature, blocks) and centers where children can play the roles they see around them.

Here's How
Because centers are most successful when geared to children's interests, consider letting some centers evolve as the year progresses rather than feeling pressure to have them all fully outfitted at the beginning of the year. Also regularly take stock of role-playing centers to see that children have props for playing those roles inspired by their studies or interests, for example, props for a bakery, a flower stand, or a doctor's office.

Field Trips and Resource People

The general purpose of early education programs is to help children better interact with and understand the world outside of the classroom. This can be accomplished in two ways: taking the children into the community and bringing the community into the classroom. When it is important to see a topic under study in its actual setting, a visit into the community is in order. Trips to the park or the zoo are interesting and enjoyable. In addition, trips to local business or agencies provide children with real-life experiences that help them better understand their community and the roles people play within it.

Here's How

Field trips into the community should be planned well in advance so that families can sign and return permission slips. It is also important to prepare children for the experience, discussing what they might see and introducing any new vocabulary associated with the trip.

Bringing the community to the children begins with children's families. Send a note home early in the school year to see what occupations are represented, what hobbies adult family members have, what musical instruments they play, and so on. Solicit their interest in sharing their expertise with the children. Having a family member visit not only expands children's knowledge and understanding of some topic, but also helps family members feel comfortable working in the classroom. A sample note to be sent home to families soliciting their involvement is provided as a reproducible blackline master in the appendix.

PART THREE

Music
of Literacy

3

Music of Literacy

The Importance of Music for Literacy Development

A growing body of research is showing significant positive correlations between systematic musical experiences for preschool children and their literacy development. (For a summary of the research, enter "relationship of music education of young children and emergent literacy" in your Web browser.) This conclusion is based on the following:

1. Musical activities are pleasant for children and create excitement for academic participation while also promoting social-emotional development.
2. Music education contributes to preschool children's awakening to different subject matters, particularly to reading, writing, and mathematics.
3. Musical activities promote the development of auditory perception, phonological memory, and metacognitive knowledge—three components that are equally involved in the development of linguistic abilities.
4. More specifically, children who have good melodic perception are better able to decode and manipulate the various linguistic units—rhymes, rhythm, syllables, phonemes, word recognition, and beginning consonant sounds.
5. Similar results emerged when an integrated music program was related to mathematics achievement, particularly in the area of spatial reasoning.

To find out more, enter the words "effects of music on preschool programs" into your Web browser. You can find summaries of the many scientific studies addressing the topic.

The Use of Music in Early Childhood Programs

Purposeful musical experiences in early childhood programs typically revolve around a number of goals:

- transitions
- singing
- movement and physical development
- music appreciation

Transitions

Transitions are the many times within the daily program when children move from one activity to another, are restless from sitting too long, or are returning from an activity outside of the classroom. Because singing is pleasurable for most children, adding this element into transitions provides a satisfying outlet. Vary the songs throughout the week and year to include the children's favorites. Happily, many of the classic children's songs also incidentally teach important concepts. Songs might include rhyming, letter or word recognition, numbers, body parts, colors, or shapes.

Using "direction" songs that relate to specific time slots is often counterproductive. The tunes are rarely melodic and soon become boring. Stopping all children at once at the end of individual playtime can have a negative effect. During this free time, children have been engaged in activities that take varying times to clean up. Stopping them all at one time means some children only have to close a book, while others might have to put away a large number of blocks. Those standing around with nothing to do sometimes get in the way of others who need to complete cleanup work. Remember, clean up by task, not by time. Start a few minutes earlier with the block group, move on to those at the easel, and then go on to the book browsers. This way, all children finish their cleanup tasks at the same time. Then, as a way of drawing everyone to the next activity, start singing one of the children's favorite songs.

Singing is not the only form of transition activity. Simple word games, clapping patterns, and movement activities are also useful. The key is to use a variety of ways to help children deal with transitions in the daily schedule—music being one of the most enjoyable.

Singing

Include a time for singing in the daily schedule. You might use singing as a transition activity, as mentioned above, but additional opportunities for singing are also important. Singing provides opportunities to help children develop musical concepts—high/low, fast/slow, loud/soft—that also enhance wider learning. The goal is enjoyment, but the learning comes from the selection of songs.

> Using songs that include direct instruction of literacy skills is not recommended. This book lists many authentic activities for teaching numbers, letters, words, and other skills. The purpose of singing is to provide an enjoyable reinforcement of those skills when done on a regular basis.

Movement and Physical Development

The purpose of a movement and physical development program is to help children increase their agility, strength, endurance, balance, and coordination using the principles of force, speed, flow, and time. While this can be accomplished through regular physical activities, incorporating music with movement-based activities adds to the enjoyment.

Music Appreciation

Music enhances children's lives. For example, the enjoyment of a beautiful fall or spring day might be reflected in singing "Oh, What a Beautiful Morning." On a rainy day, singing "Raindrops Keep Fallin' on My Head" has a similar impact. Listening to classical music has been shown to lead to at least temporary gains in the brain's ability to process information. (For a summary of the research, enter "relationship of classical music to young children's brain functioning" in your Web browser.) Plenty of wonderful recordings of "Peter and the Wolf" by Prokofiev and of pieces by Mozart, as well as the various efforts by pop orchestras on behalf of children, show the popularity of exposing children to classical music.

Talk with children about how music helps express feelings, and then demonstrate that through the music you expose them to. Music is also an enjoyable way to expand children's understanding of other cultures. Listening to music from countries around the world can help students acquire a multicultural perspective.

The Value of Song Charts

Many teachers create song charts, which combine words and pictures to represent the lyrics of songs. A sample song chart is shown on page 83. Song charts help children in the following ways:

- Charts help children learn a song by providing clues.
- Charts promote success for all children because of the use of two code systems—picture and word.
- Charts help children remember the sequence in accumulative songs, for example, "There Was an Old Woman Who Swallowed a Fly." Try highlighting the repeated phrases in these songs by writing them in a different color or underlining them.
- Charts help children see the relationship between pictures and words as they identify objects in a song.
- Charts help children develop a sense of word identification and rhyme through repeated singing of each song throughout the year.
- Charts can be reproduced and taken home by children, who can then successfully teach the songs to their family members.
- Charts also help teachers learn and remember songs as they teach them to children.

When you use a song chart, cover the pictures from time to time so that children can focus on the words. Cover and uncover the pictures during the year to make sure all children feel comfortable. By the end of the year, children will know the songs both from memory and by recognizing the words.

Introducing a New Song

Learning a new song should occur over time. Learning songs line by line in rote fashion is neither enjoyable for the children nor useful in teaching skills. The task of mastering a new song over a period of time makes singing a real pleasure, and the subsequent mastery of any attendant skills becomes a fortunate consequence.

When using a song chart to introduce a new song, follow these steps:

1. Show the children the chart.
2. Introduce the key words and pictures.
3. Sing the song while pointing to the appropriate words and pictures.
4. Ask the children to join you in singing the song several times.
5. Then, stop the work on the new song and continue singing other songs the children know already.
6. Repeat this process frequently until the children learn the new song. Once they know it, make the melody and lyrics a part of their regular singing program.

Where to Find Music for Early Childhood Programs

We have provided song charts and lyrics for several songs on the following pages; however, an extensive collection of children's music is necessary to maintain an effective music program. The collection should include a wide variety of music to meet the desired outcomes for listening, singing, and movement. There are many sources of music for classroom use.

Audiotapes and CDs

Audiotapes and CDs are the most common sources of music for children. These may be found in libraries, in retail stores, and at community sales. Some popular artists include Raffi, Hap Palmer, Jim Gill, Fred Koch, Debbie Clement, and Justin Roberts. You can also find compilations featuring many artists on a single CD or tape. Some compilations are themed and may feature music for holidays, classical selections, lullabies, or songs from cultures around the world.

Long-Playing (33 ⅓ rpm) Records

These "gems" are still available in used record shops and at community sales. Many children's recording artists—Ella Jenkins, Pete Seeger, Burl Ives, Oscar Brand, and others—got their start during the LP generation. Besides being less expensive, LPs are designed for teachers and children to find the songs much more easily than on tapes and CDs. LP record players are now back on the market, and can be purchased with LP, tape, and CD formats all in one device. LP record players are also available in secondhand stores and at community sales. Make sure they are in working condition before you make your purchase.

The Internet

Modern technology has made music easily available to early childhood teachers. You can access songs from the Internet by typing "lyrics and music for (the song title)" into your Web browser. Try "I Can Sing a Rainbow lyrics," for example. You will be given a list of Web sites where you can access the words and music.

Alternately, you can go to www.niehs.nih.gov/kids/musicchild.htm, which contains an extensive song list maintained by the National Institute of Environmental Health Sciences. Click on a title to see the words and to hear the song. These songs can be downloaded if they are used for educational purposes. If you have a computer in the classroom, the children can sing along. If you are using the computer for research, you can learn the song and then teach it to the children.

Hush, Little Baby

MOCKINGBIRD

DIAMOND RING

LOOKING GLASS

BILLY GOAT

Hush, Little Baby

And if that diamond ring turns brass,
Mama's gonna buy you a looking glass.
And if that looking glass gets broke,
Papa's gonna buy you a billy goat.
And if that billy goat won't pull,
Mama's gonna buy you a cart and bull.
And if that cart and bull turn over,
Papa's gonna buy you a dog named Rover.
And if that dog named Rover won't bark,
Mama's gonna buy you a horse and cart.
And if that horse and cart fall down,
You'll still be the sweetest little baby in town.

Pretty Colors
Sung to the tune of "Clementine"

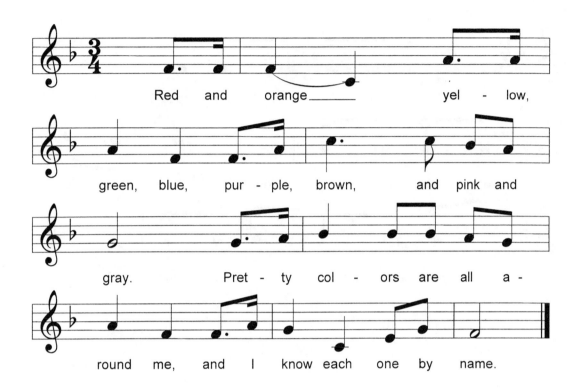

Red and orange_____ yel - low,
green, blue, pur - ple, brown, and pink and
gray. Pret - ty col - ors are all a -
round me, and I know each one by name.

Who Is Wearing . . . ?
Sung to the tune of "Farmer in the Dell"

Oh, who is wear - ing red? Oh,

who is wear - ing red? Please tell me

if you can. Oh, who is wear - ing red?

Oh, Sam is wearing red.

Oh, Sam is wearing red.

That's the color of his shirt.

Oh, Sam is wearing red.

Continue singing, changing the color name, the child's name, and the name of the article of clothing.

If You Are Wearing . . .
Sung to the tune of "If You're Happy and You Know It"

If you are wearing blue, touch your shoe.
If you are wearing blue, touch your shoe.
If you are wearing blue, then please
touch your shoe.
If you are wearing blue, touch your shoe.

If you are wearing black, pat your back.
If you are wearing black, pat your back.
If you are wearing black, then please pat
your back.
If you are wearing black, pat your back.

If you are wearing brown, turn around.
If you are wearing brown, turn around.
If you are wearing brown, then please
turn around.
If you are wearing brown, turn around.

Continue adding other verses with colors and rhyming actions.

This Old Man

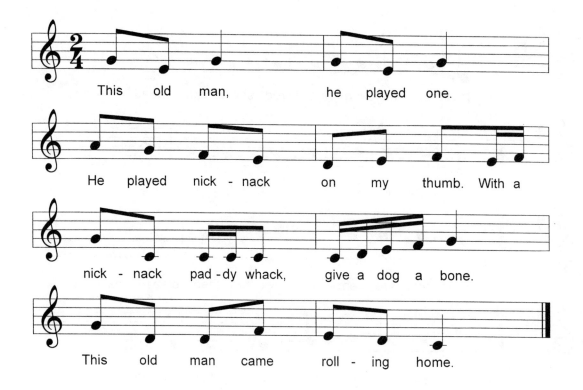

Continue singing the verses for the numbers two through ten,
using these rhymes:

two—shoe	five—hive	eight—at my gate
three—knee	six—sticks	nine—on my spine
four—floor	seven—up in heaven	ten—once again

Ten in the Bed

Continue singing, counting down each verse until the final verse:
There was one in the bed, and the little one said, "Good night!"

Ten Little Sailors

Old Da-vey Jones had one lit-tle sail-or,

Old Da-vey Jones had one lit-tle sail-or,

Old Da-vey Jones had one lit-tle sail-or

One lit-tle sail-or boy._____ He had

one, he had two, he had three lit-tle sail-ors,

Four, he had five, he had six lit-tle sail-ors,

Sev-en, he had eight, he had nine lit-tle sail-ors,

Ten lit-tle sail-or boys._____

Sing the song again, this time counting down from ten:

Old Davey Jones had ten little sailors,
Old Davey Jones had ten little sailors,
Old Davey Jones had ten little sailors,
Ten little sailor boys.

He had ten, he had nine, he had
    eight little sailors,
Seven he had, six he had, five little sailors,
Four he had, three he had, two little sailors,
One little sailor boy.

Head and Shoulders, Knees and Toes
Sung to the tune of "London Bridge"

Head   and   shoul - ders,   knees   and   toes,

knees   and   toes,   knees   and   toes.

Head   and   shoul - ders   knees   and   toes,   we

all   stand   up   to - geth - er. _____

Eyes and ears and mouth and nose,

Mouth and nose,

Mouth and nose,

Eyes and ears and mouth and nose,

We all stand up together.

Ankles, elbows, feet and seat,

Feet and seat,

Feet and seat,

Ankles, elbows, feet and seat,

We all stand up together.

The Hokey Pokey

*Keep singing using other body parts, such as left hand, right foot,
left foot, big head, backside, whole self.*

The Alphabet Song

B-I-N-G-O

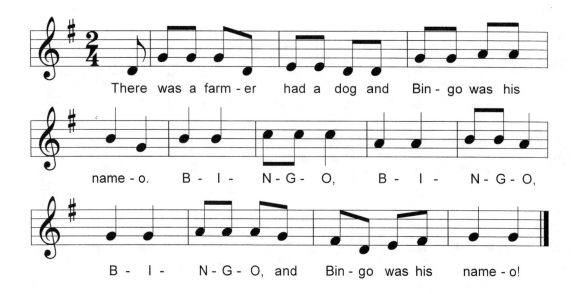

Continue singing, only with each successive verse, replace one letter
at a time in B-I-N-G-O with a clap, rather than saying the letter.
At the end of the song, you will be clapping five times.

Old MacDonald Had a Farm

Old Mac-Don-ald had a farm, E - I - E - I -

O. And on that farm he had some chicks,

E - I - E - I - O. With a chick-chick here, and a

chick - chick there, here a chick, there a chick

ev -'ry -where a chick - chick. Old Mac - Don - ald

had a farm, E - I - E - I - O.

Continue singing, adding a new animal name and sound for each verse while also keeping the previous names and sounds, building a cumulative song. Examples include:

cow—moo, moo

pig—snort, snort

horse—neigh, neigh

Itsy, Bitsy Spider

PART FOUR

Connecting
with the Home

4

Connecting with the Home

Research has confirmed that a positive and active home-school partnership is a powerful tool in children's learning. (For a summary of the research, enter "relationship between parent involvement in young children's education and children's achievement" in your Web browser.)

Although families of young children have many competing pressures that surround their important job of nurturing, supporting, and parenting, it is the school's responsibility to make sure that families are invited into the learning program and have many opportunities to participate. Here are some ideas about how to make that happen.

Successful Strategies for Working with Families

1. Let families know that reading to their children on a daily basis is an activity that is easy yet of critical importance. Children who are regularly read to beginning at birth and involved in story-related discussions exhibit higher reading achievement and aptitude in later school programs than children who are not read to. Provide families with information on how to read to children. (In the appendix, we have provided a tip sheet that you can send home to parents.)

2. At the start of the school year, give each family a copy of their child's Individual Profile so they are aware of the emergent literacy areas in which their child will be involved. Even though some families may not read the profile, it is the program's responsibility to keep them informed. It is the families' right to use the information as they choose.

3. Organize a meeting early in the year to talk with each child's family about the entire program and how they can help their child. Offer babysitting as an incentive, and set aside a separate room for the children and babysitter to occupy while the families meet with you. Prepare handouts (in home languages when needed) so families don't have to rely on their memory. Keep the meeting short and plan carefully so you can cover your points and allow time for general questions. At the end of the meeting, indicate your willingness to set up additional meetings with families who have personal questions about their children. Also, encourage families to call you when they have a question.

4. Share individual children's progress with their families regularly. This can be accomplished in several ways:

- Provide regular updates in the form of a weekly or biweekly letter sent home. (We have provided a Sample Family Letter on page 103.) You can tell families about
  a. the upcoming theme or unit of study;
  b. some of the major activities;
  c. related activities that they can be involved in at home;
  d. suggestions for related home materials that can be shared with the classroom;
  e. possibilities for parents to share related stories from their lives, jobs, and so on.
- Send periodic notes to families sharing something interesting their child did in class or something humorous the child said. Families always appreciate this personal touch.
- Every three months, send home a written summary of their child's progress along with specific suggestions for follow-up activities at home. Some teachers say they provide this information verbally, as needed, on a regular basis as families drop off or pick up their children. However, this form of communication relies on memory. Remember, the person picking up the child is only one part of the home-school partnership. It is the program's responsibility to provide all involved parties with important information about their children's progress.
- Schedule a spring and fall conference where families can discuss all aspects of their child's school experience. This conference should cover four topics:

   a. specific areas where a child has demonstrated strengths

   b. specific areas where a child has demonstrated needs

   c. specific activities in which families can support children
       at home in their areas of need

   d. questions about the child or the program from families, as
       well as information they'd like to share about their child

5. Regularly collect student work samples and have them available
    at conference times so families can see work that represents their
    child's progress.

6. Call special conference times when there is a need to discuss
    certain aspects of a child's progress or behavior. Of course, the
    goal is that things will change or improve before families need
    to get involved; it may not seem appropriate to involve families
    until there has been a diagnosis of important learning issues or
    social behaviors. Once a problem is evident, however, it is crucial
    to discuss this with the family. Perhaps a serious family situation
    has come up, or perhaps you are dealing with a potential health
    or psychological problem. Once the problem has been clearly
    defined, you can better identify ways the program can help solve
    the problem. Defining the problem may also lead to a referral to
    other professionals inside or outside the program.

7. Periodically send letters home highlighting several outcomes you
    wish families to reinforce—predicting and retelling stories, for
    example. Provide families with specific directions so they can be
    successful.

8. Understand that family responses to your efforts will vary from
    high interest and involvement to little interest and no involve-
    ment. All you can do is provide the opportunities; you cannot be
    responsible for those who choose to remain uninvolved.

9. Invite adult family members to serve as resource persons to
    provide firsthand stories about something in their child's life,
    to play a musical instrument for the children's enjoyment, or to
    share hobbies and collections. These are all enriching experi-
    ences for children. To gather this information, send home a brief
    survey asking families to list interests, hobbies, and other unique
    experiences and then schedule short visits during the year. (We
    have provided a sample letter in the appendix.)

10. Make families aware that there are opportunities to assist in the
    classroom. Identify specific jobs parents can be engaged in—
    both clerical and educational. This distinction is important.
    Some adults enjoy being in the classroom but only want jobs

such as setting up snacks or making new bulletin boards. Others enjoy reading to or playing games with children. Send a note home listing the kinds of jobs available and how often help is needed. Encourage short visits, one or two days a week—which may be more practical for them to schedule. Adult family members who work in the classroom have a greater appreciation of the work of the teachers and a greater understanding of how their child fits into the program.

11. Accept the individual differences inherent in all individuals. Some family members are shy while others are overly demanding. Some appreciate everything you do for them and their child while others appear critical of your efforts. Some provide lots of support by sending items to school and working with their child at home while others appear too busy or uncaring. Treat families in the same way you treat a group of children:

- Accept individual differences for what they are; you can't change anyone's behavior in a short period of time.
- Continue to provide opportunities for families to partner with the program.
- Be content with the parent and family responses you do receive.
- Do not let any negative relationships with families affect your relationship with their children.

Sample Family Letter

January 2011

Dear Families,

We have completed our midterm assessment and have found that there are some areas in which you can easily work with your child at home. The key is to make these experiences easy and enjoyable so both you and your child look forward to them.

1. Continue to read to your child daily.

2. Help your child learn to write her first name.

3. Help your child learn the letters in his first name. At times, print the letters out of order when doing this task. For example, if Carlos is your child's first name, have him find the letters *r c o s a l* in his name and in the names of your other family members.

4. Be sure your child knows her full name and address.

5. Tell your child about the emergency 911 telephone number (this could be important to your family's health and safety in an emergency).

If you have any questions, please see me when you bring your child to the program or call me at 555-0129.

Thank you for helping your child with these important tasks.

Sincerely yours,

Elise Weaver

PART FIVE

Lesson

Activities

5

Lesson Activities

It's a good idea to familiarize yourself with all twenty-eight lesson activities before beginning the year. Many of the activity ideas can be implemented across your lessons, during choice time, and in individual or group settings. Spontaneously employing the ideas greatly contributes to meeting the outcomes involved. Additionally, many lesson activities suggest things that you can do to prepare your room at the beginning of the year.

Lesson activities 1 through 18, and their attendant outcomes, should receive the bulk of your attention during the fall months. Nevertheless, lesson activities 19 through 28 should certainly be a part of your overall planning as well. For example, retelling stories (lesson activity 20) can naturally occur whenever you are reading with the children. If you have familiarized yourself with the activities in that lesson, implementing the ideas when appropriate will come naturally to you.

Each lesson activity is tied directly to an outcome that appears on the Individual Profile and the Group Profile sheets included with this program. Therefore, as you implement the activity ideas, remember that your observations of individual children might reveal breakthroughs that you can record on the profiles.

Lesson Activity 1

Outcome: Knows first and last name

Most children enter preschool (age three) knowing their first name, and many also know their last name. However, many of these same children enter preschool unable to recognize their first and last names in print. Therefore, it is important to display children's first and last names in the classroom, but always in a way related to some aspect of the daily program. Some examples of ways to do this are listed below.

Activities

Name Chart

Make and display a chart with the children's first and last names. Refer to the chart frequently throughout the year. For example, look for common names and names that look similar to others—Jon and John. Discuss with the children which parts of the names are different.

Name Games

Help the children examine the names and identify similar names and/or initial sounds. Look for the longest and shortest names and names that begin with the same letter. Make up rhyming words for names, even using nonsense words.

Seat Labels

Tape the first name and first letter of each child's last name to his individual seating space. Completely cover the names with wide, clear tape so they remain affixed. This helps the children identify their seats. Switch the class seating regularly to initiate new social interactions.

Name-Card Game

Periodically play Switch Places, a game using name cards. Early in the year, you can also include photos. To play Switch Places, have the children sit in a circle, and hold the name cards in your hand. Sometimes use first names, and sometimes use last names. Hold up two cards and, without saying the names, ask those children to change places in the circle. Initially, let other children help. Play each game until all names have been exchanged. As the year goes on, eliminate the photos and only let other children help when a child asks for assistance. For those children having difficulty recognizing their names, work with them independently to foster success.

Check-In Fun

Make check-in sticks for independent roll call. (See Individual Attendance Devices in the Classroom Essentials section for additional details and options.) Write the children's names on a tongue depressor, and then have the children draw their faces and cut out their drawings. Attach the drawing of each child's face to a tongue depressor labeled with the child's name. As the children arrive at the program each day, have them find their check-in sticks (they will recognize their drawings at first) and put them in the "here" box. Eventually the children will begin to recognize their names. Photos can replace the drawings, and eventually the names can stand alone as the children become proficient in recognizing their names in print.

Label Their Work

Until children can correctly write their complete first names, write their names on the back or front of all individual work. This helps the children gain ownership of their work as they continue to see their names in print.

Helpers Chart

Construct a helpers chart using a blank calendar grid. (See Helpers Charts in the Classroom Essentials sections for additional details and options.) Identify each month and insert the appropriate dates. Put a list of the regular tasks for which the helpers are responsible and announce special tasks as they arise. Select two helpers per day so that those children are involved in many tasks. At first, use written names and photos to help children make an immediate connection to their assigned days. Remove the photos as the children begin to recognize their written names. Early in the school year, remind the children of their tasks, but then expect them to take greater responsibility over the course of the year.

Photo Captions

Construct a photos-of-classmates chart. Display an enlarged group photo of all the children and write the names of the children in order of their appearance. Have small copies of the enlarged photo made to give to each child when they are able to name all of their classmates.

Book of Friends

Have the children draw a self-portrait on a sheet of paper, and then have them write/scribble their names on the bottom line. Print their names on the top of the sheet. If available, add each child's photo. Make additional copies of each child's self-portrait, add a title page, and (with the children) assemble a Book of Friends to take home.

Name Chant

Use a call-and-response style of chant to review names. Make up a simple tune if you'd like.

Teacher: Whose name is _____(Charlie)?

Child: My name is _____ (Charlie).

Continue until all children have been named. You can also sing another version using last names. As the children's familiarity with one another's names grows, you can do the chant as a chain rather than having the teacher lead every time.

Lesson Activity 2

Outcome: Writes first name and first letter of last name

Because the majority of four-year-olds will not be able to write their names, begin to work on name writing as soon as possible. Encourage the children to write their names often, using whatever stage of writing they are in—scribbling, writing the first letter, or printing. Remember that this is an ongoing program goal and that children will show varied individual growth. Develop the skill through a variety of activities, such as those described below, throughout the program year.

Activities

My Teacher

Have children create teacher images (see Teacher Photos in the Classroom Essentials section) during the first week of the fall program. Accept their drawings and whatever symbols they write for their names. This activity is the start of picture writing and alphabet writing. Have the children take the teacher pictures home to be placed on a family bulletin board or in the children's own space. Teachers should be sure to closely examine the pages before they go home, because they serve a major purpose. This activity is an assessment tool for the teacher to record children's knowledge of and ability to draw body parts and their ability to do initial writing.

This Is My Work

Tell the children to write their names on all personal work, emphasizing at least the first letter of each child's first name. Accept whatever form the symbol takes. This is the start of the children's ability to write their names, and it will take some time for them to develop proficiency. The teacher should also write each child's name on the sheet.

Name Tracing

Regularly have the children trace over their names that you have written out for them. Provide them with lightweight paper that allows the name to show through clearly. Let the children select their favorite crayon color and encourage them to change colors from time to time. Keep copies in each child's portfolio as evidence of growth or of the need for individual assistance.

Name Folders

This activity is best for working with children during choice time. Construct some transparent pocket folders on which children can practice writing their names with erasable markers. Staple clear transparencies over the front of each manila folder (one for each child), leaving the top free so you can insert sheets of paper. For each child, prepare individual sheets with several varieties of their names, such as

- their first name and the first letter of their last name written in dots they can connect to form letters;
- their first name and the first letter of their last name written in alphabet letters, with ample space below where children can copy the letters;
- their name written with blanks for missing letters they have to fill in.

Insert the sheets into the folder so the children can practice on the transparency. The reusable folder helps save a lot of paper.

Choice Time, Practice Time

Work with individual children who show an interest in writing their names. Have paper and writing materials available during choice time.

Writing to Check In

As the year progresses, replace the check-in devices by having children write their names as they arrive each morning.

Lesson Activity 3

Outcome: Repeats home address

Children first entering preschool cannot be expected to remember their full house number, street name, and city; however, they should know their full address by the end of the school year. This is important for several reasons. Children come to know that their home has an identification that is unique. They also learn the different components of an address and are prepared to provide their address should they become lost.

Activities

Map It

Provide state and local maps for reference. On a local area map, put pins into the locations where children in the class live. Measure the distances from the homes to the school to see who lives the closest and the farthest. Talk about how the children come to school—by walking, by automobile, or by public transportation. Send families a note asking them to provide you with the amount of time it takes to travel with their child to school one way. Chart this on a bar graph, and relate the data to the distances on the map.

Our Address Book

On a small piece of paper or note card, write each child's name and address. Add a small photo of each child. This personalizes each address. Bind the entries together to create a small class address book.

Our Address Chart

Using posterboard, construct a chart showing each child's name and complete address. The headers across the top of the chart should be the following parts of an address:

> family name
> house number and street name
> apartment or condo number
> city
> state
> ZIP code

Help the children identify the different parts of their addresses. Look for similar street names, area codes, and numbers. From time to time, ask the children if they can tell you the parts of an address. Let them help each other with the challenge. Note: don't concentrate on the ZIP code at this stage of learning. Simply point out that this code is used by the postal workers to deliver mail.

The Parts of a Home

Ask each child to draw a picture of her home. Talk about the walls, the roof, the doors, and the windows. Have some examples of the outsides of different types of homes handy for reference. When the children have completed their work, write the correct house number on the front door of each child's house.

Broadening the Area

Make regular reference to the community and the state in which your program is located.

Lesson Activity 4

Outcome: Knows purpose of and can dial 911

This is an important outcome for children to master. When children know how to call 911 in an emergency, they might someday save a life.

Activities

911 Basics

Discuss with children the fact that the 911 emergency line exists. Make them aware that the calls to 911 should only be emergency calls where someone's life or home is in real danger. Give examples of times when calling 911 is appropriate (someone is very sick, there is a fire in a home or garage, there has been an automobile accident) and when it is inappropriate ("I can't find my doll."). Discuss why proper use of 911 is so important, and tell them that 911 is set up to provide immediate help in an emergency. Remind them that help might be delayed by people calling in when it is not appropriate.

Real Stories

Share news articles that deal with how someone was helped because of a call to 911.

Real Professionals

If you have access to resource people within the community (firefighters, police officers, 911 operators), ask them to come in to talk with the children. They can provide examples of how the 911 system works. Ask them to highlight the kinds of calls they receive that are not appropriate.

Position of the Numbers on the Phone

Make a poster of a telephone keypad so the children can see the location of the 9 and the 1. Have the children come to the poster and press the 9 once and then the 1 twice. Explain that the 9 and 1 might look different on different phones. Show examples using pictures, cordless phones, office phones, and cell phones.

Practice Dialing

Bring a disconnected telephone into the classroom and let the children practice keying in the numbers. The telephone company is a source for free old telephones that they disable for educational use. Parents might also have phones at home they are not currently using.

Talking to the Operator

Prepare children for the types of questions they'll be asked if they ever call 911. Let them know they'll give their name and then they'll tell the operator what the emergency is. Tell them that the 911 operator will ask for the address, which is another reason why learning their home address is so important for the children. Point out that they should not hang up the phone, but stay on the line as long as possible. Emphasize speaking clearly and loudly.

Lesson Activity 5
Outcome: Recognizes eleven basic colors

Most children enter preschool knowing several color names. Helping them know a common set of colors expands their use of colors in the classroom and their awareness of colors in their environment. Because colors are so much a part of our everyday world, most children will quickly learn their basic colors. There is little need for direct instruction on this outcome.

Activities

Color Names
Find ways each day to use a color name in classroom materials and activities. Post a color chart in the room for handy reference. Frequent use of color names throughout all parts of the daily program will help the children learn color names and refer to them when working on their own.

Colors in Songs
To introduce and review colors, use the song "Pretty Colors" (provided in the Music of Literacy section) and a visual element made up of separate strips of the colors named in the song. As children first learn the song, point to each color at the appropriate time. Move the colors around between singing times to be sure children don't just memorize the placement of the colors, rather than learning to recognize the colors themselves. Later, have the children point to the colors, or distribute the strips and have the children raise them at the right times as you sing. Note: several other color-oriented songs are included in the Music of Literacy section. Singing about colors at random times is great natural reinforcement of color lessons.

Colors in the Environment
Help the children identify colors in their environment, such as those associated with different holidays, colors of favorite local or national sports teams, colors used on logos of local businesses, the colors of traffic signals and signs, and so on.

Books about Colors

Feature books that focus on colors. Here are a few favorites of parents and teachers:

- *Chuck Murphy's Color Surprises: A Pop-Up Book* by Chuck Murphy (1997). This simple yet beautiful book features a square of one color on each page. Each square pops up to reveal an amazing animal of that color.
- *Red Is a Dragon: A Book of Colors* by Roseanne Thong and Grace Lin (2001). Children learn about Asian-American culture while also learning colors.
- *A Color of His Own* by Leo Lionni (2003). This delightful book about a chameleon teaches the colors but also includes a wonderful life lesson.
- *My Many Colored Days* by Dr. Seuss, Steve Johnson, and Lou Fancher (1998). Only brought to life after Dr. Suess's death, this book links colors to feelings.
- *Planting a Rainbow* by Lois Ehlert (2003). Readers follow the planting of a family garden in which all the colors of the rainbow are represented.

Color Collages

Help the children make color collages highlighting individual colors. For example, have magazines available for children to cut out all the blue colors they can find and then paste them into a poster. This activity helps children see that one color contains many hues and shades.

Shades of Color

Obtain color chips from a paint store to show children the different shades of color. Have them look at the paint samples to see when a shade of color turns into another color.

Mixing Colors

Show children how mixing colors makes new colors; for example, mixing red and yellow makes orange. The fun books *Mouse Paint* by Ellen Stoll Walsh (2006) and *White Rabbit's Color Book* by Alan Baker (2003) are both about mixing colors.

My Favorite Color

Construct a graph of the children's favorite colors. Revisit the graph periodically throughout the year to see how children's color preferences may have changed. Make a badge for each child with his favorite color to be worn on certain days. Ask children to look at one another's badges and identify the colors. At times, change the badge colors or use color combinations, continuing this activity until most of the children know their colors. You can also wear some unique color badges to stretch the children's color recognition and vocabulary. Have paint chips available for children to use in identifying your colors. Add these to the color chart for continued identification but not for assessment.

Color Games
Play group games such as Simon Says or Red Rover, Red Rover, giving color commands, such as "Simon says sit down if you are wearing something red" or "Red rover, red rover, everyone wearing blue comes over."

Lesson Activity 6

Outcome: Counts from 1 to 31

Many children enter preschool with some basic number concepts, primarily in reference to their age. Some children can verbalize their age, while others hold up fingers to indicate the number. Some children can do rote counting but are not aware of counting as a useful activity. Just the regular and effective use of a calendar will enable children to count to 31 by the end of the program year. The key to successful attainment of this outcome is involvement of children in many daily counting activities for useful purposes.

With regard to counting early in the year, do not be concerned whether or not all of the children can actually count. You can count and invite the children to join in. Some can follow for a few numbers, and some drop off quickly. The principle at work is *useful repetition*. As the class counts a variety of useful items daily, individual children will be able to name more numbers over time.

Activities

What's in the Bag?

After assessing children at the start of the year, fill baggies with a varied number of items (such as crayons, pencils, beads, and so on). Periodically ask individual children to count the items. Make notes on the assessment sheets about their level of growth.

How Many Days Until . . . ?

Using the calendar described in Effective Calendars in the Classroom Essentials section, count how many days are left before the occurrence of special events, holidays, birthdays, parent meetings, field trips, and other important dates. In the early part of the year, you will just start counting as a normal activity. Let the children join you to the extent they can. At times, start counting but then stop to see how well the children continue to count. Tell the children that you would like them to count to the designated date, and then help them as needed.

Interactive Monthly Chart

Construct a How-many-days-have-we-been-in-school? chart, adding a new number each day. Fill in the chart for the first week or so, and then ask children who are interested to add numbers for the next days. Ask them to tell you each number, then ask them how they will write it.

Make sure the chart has correct numbers to look back on so the children can use it to anticipate each new number.

I'll Wait

Construct an I'll Wait Timeline so that the class can count backward in anticipation of an event. (See An I'll Wait Timeline in the Classroom Essentials section for complete guidelines.) Discuss with the children their excitement about special events and how they're always wondering how many days there are until a special day. Make a list of exciting events the children are looking forward to. Introduce the I'll Wait Timeline related to an event that will occur within the next week and show the children how you will slide the number line each day until the event has arrived. This allows children to anticipate the future and count backward to that time.

Counting in Music and Literature

Many familiar songs and beloved children's books feature counting as part of the lyrics and story line. Singing and reading are fun ways to incidentally work on counting. For example, in the Music of Literacy section of this book, we have included the songs "This Old Man," "Ten in the Bed," and "Ten Little Sailors." Some examples of classic counting books include *Fish Eyes: A Book You Can Count On* by Lois Ehlert (2001), *Five Little Ducks* by Raffi, illustrated by Jose Aruego and Ariane Dewey (2000), and *Mouse Count* by Ellen Stoll Walsh (2006).

Individual Counting

Work with individual children who need help. For example, during choice time, ask them to count items in their center; take them to the calendar and count upcoming events; or ask them to count up to their age. Learning to count can be achieved by counting items in the classroom environment.

Lesson Activity 7

Outcome: Recognizes numerals 1 to 10 out of order

As children learn to say their numbers, they are emphasizing the number names, and they are learning the sequence of numbers when they count. However, this is only part of the task in beginning to use numbers in their lives. The next phase is learning to recognize numerals and to identify their proper names. Most often these two outcomes will be accomplished together.

Activities

Establishing Level of Proficiency

Administer the Numeral Recognition assessment found in the Assessment section to children individually. The numbers 1 to 10 have been randomly placed on a sheet of paper. Point to each number and ask the child to identify the numeral. Record the results on the assessment sheet. Based on that information, provide a variety of individual and group activities.

Number Charts

As suggested in Alphabet and Number Charts in the Classroom Essentials section, you should display a number chart in the room. This way, you can refer to numbers and their names as needed.

Telephone Numbers

Help the children understand why it is important to know their telephone number. On sturdy card stock, write each child's telephone number. Send the cards home with children so parents can help them with this activity. (Many families might also want their children to know certain cell phone numbers so children can reach them when needed.)

Number Line

Make number cards for the numerals 1 through 10 and put them in a sealable plastic bag with a 1 through 10 number line also enclosed. Put a line across the bottom of each number card so children will know which is right side up. Have children try to put the cards in numerical order along the line, saying each number name.

Numbers Game

Play Number Concentration. Make Number Concentration cards (or use a deck of playing cards) by numbering two sets of ten cards from 1 to 10. As you start out, the game is best played with a small group of children.

Eventually some children will be able to play the game with a partner or by themselves. Shuffle the cards and lay them face down on the table so they are not touching. The first child picks up two cards. If they are a pair, the child keeps them. If they are not a pair, the cards are returned to the table in their places. The next child does the same thing. When all the cards have been paired, the child with the most pairs is the winner. While there is an element of luck in this game, the test is for the children to remember the location of cards that have been revealed but then put back on the table.

Did I Count That Right?

Periodically "test" the children by counting some objects out of order. If no one catches the error, have children count the objects as a group. Have them compare that number with the incorrect number.

Measure It!

Let the children help with tasks that involve measurement, such as cooking. Be sure to use a variety of measuring devices in the program— a ruler, yardstick, tape measure, and measuring cups and spoons, for example.

Data Collection

Use the grid described in Data-Collecting Activities in the Classroom Essentials section to collect data about things such as the children's favorite colors, favorite ice-cream flavors, and eye colors. Children can count the results in each column and then determine the differences among the columns. This is an activity children enjoy because it lets them suggest their favorites and then compare them with the favorites of others. You can continue this activity throughout the year even after the children have learned to recognize the numbers.

Books about Numbers

Feature books that focus on numbers. Here are a few favorites of parents and teachers:

- *10 Little Rubber Ducks* by Eric Carle (2005). Carle teaches so much in his beautiful books, and his approach to ordinal numbers is considered by many to be his finest effort. The story is based on something that really happened, which adds to the charm.
- *I Spy Little Numbers* by Jean Marzollo and Walter Wick (1999). A part of the I Spy Little Book series, this book features rhymes and bright colors to help children learn the numbers.
- *Little Rabbit's First Number Book* by Alan Baker and Kate Petty (1998). Reviewers are especially fond of book because it leads to an

understanding of numbers rather than straight memorization.

* *Zin! Zin! Zin! A Violin* by Lloyd Moss and Marjorie Priceman (1995). This out-of-the-ordinary book teaches readers about an orchestra while also giving them a new way to understand numbers. Written in rhyme and wonderfully illustrated, this book will endlessly enchant many children.

Numbers All Around

Environmental print features many numbers. Make a list of the many ways numbers are on display in the environment—on telephones, in recipes, as parts of addresses, on speed-limit signs, to show prices, and so on. Leave space for the children to add items as they discover them. Have newspapers and magazines available for them to browse through for additional ideas.

Lesson Activity 8

Outcome: Demonstrates an understanding of one-to-one correspondence

One-to-one correspondence is the linking of one number with each item in a series of objects. It is a huge mental jump to go from rote counting to understanding that a number stands for a quantity, or a number of things. This skill must be modeled and directly taught, using activities in which children are involved throughout the daily schedule. The understanding of one-to-one correspondence builds from the previously mentioned counting activities—numbers on a calendar represent the number of days in a month, and check-in sticks represent how many children are present and how many are absent that day.

Activities

Our Birthdays

As described in the Yearlong Birthday Calendar in the Classroom Essentials section, construct a graph showing the months in which the children were born. Count to see how many were born in each month. Reinforce that each birthday is a special day in a specific month.

Our Names

Using the name chart that you created and posted for Lesson Activity 1, have the children count the number of letters in each of their names. Which names are the longest? Which names are the shortest?

Do the Rows Match?

Lay out two rows of small items, such as coins or blocks, so that the length of the two rows is even. Ask the children if there are the same number of items in each row, then count the items to verify. While talking about the children's answers, casually stretch out one of the lines. Again, ask the children which row has the most items. Count and verify. Discuss why it is important to count rather than to make assumptions. If you place the items on a piece of paper, you can have the children draw lines across to each corresponding item.

Count It

In choice activities, find ways to have children use counting. For example, you might ask questions, such as "How many cups of sand go into the pail?" or "How many blocks does it take to build a simple house?"

What's Your Number?

Gather cards representing the numerals 1 to 10. These can be regular playing cards or teacher-made cards. Have the children draw a card and look around the room to identify items representing the number. Have them collect the number of items to show to the other children (and as a means of teacher assessment). Pair children who need additional work with those who grasp the concept.

Helpers Using Numbers

Helpers can be thinking about one-to-one correspondence as they assist in setting-up activities. For an art activity, you might ask them to put out one box of crayons for each child, one pair of scissors for each child, one piece of paper for each child, and so on. You might specify that each child needs one, two, or three books at a table. Helpers might also use numbers as they assist in setting up for snacks. You could ask them to gather one napkin and one snack for each child at the table, for example.

How Many Buttons?

After children have begun to recognize and identify numbers, put them in a circle with a tub of buttons in the middle of the group. Give each child a number card from 1 to 10 that also includes a corresponding number of small circles. Ask each child to count out the number of buttons on the card. The child can accomplish the task in one of two ways. One is to count out the number mentally. The other is to place the buttons on the circles on the card.

Moving with Numbers

Periodically hold up a numeral and instruct the children to clap, hop, jump, or move in other ways the number of times shown.

How Many?

Periodically "test" the children's knowledge of this concept. Begin counting a number of items using your finger or other pointer. Skip an item to see if the children notice, or count an item twice in the progression. Continue this experience with individual children who need more work understanding the concept.

Lesson Activity 9

Outcome: Recites the alphabet

Children enter preschool programs with varying abilities to recite the alphabet. The basic alphabet chant is one learned early in many homes. Knowing the alphabet does not guarantee that the children can identify letters. (Letter identification is covered in another outcome.) Also, knowing the alphabet is not knowing how to read, as some parents mistakenly believe. The main purpose for learning the alphabet is to enable children to name the twenty-six letters out of order. Memorizing the alphabet provides children with an enjoyable rote learning experience, which, in most alphabet songs, also gives them an initial experience in rhyming.

Activities

Musical Alphabet

Sing "The Alphabet Song," included in the Music of Literacy section of this book. Other songs featuring the alphabet in this section include "B-I-N-G-O" and "Old MacDonald Had a Farm."

Alphabet Chart

As suggested in Alphabet and Number Charts in the Classroom Essentials section, post an alphabet chart. This can be used to help children repeat the alphabet. At times, have them try to say the alphabet backward as you point to each letter for reinforcement.

The Alphabet in Books

Read alphabet books to children and include several of them in your literacy center. You can find books that correspond to all types of themes, such as animals, holidays, places, and people.

My Own Alphabet Book

Help each child make a personalized alphabet book to take home. Write each of the alphabet letters in block form on a piece of paper, and reproduce the sheets for the number of children in the group. Let the children carefully color inside each block letter so that the letter is still recognizable. Make a cover, collate the pages, and send the books home for children to use with their families.

Extend the Learning

Work the children's basic knowledge of the alphabet into the activities suggested for Lesson Activity 10. To meet the outcomes, encourage the children to learn ten alphabet letters out of order.

Lesson Activity 10

Outcome: Identifies at least ten uppercase letters out of order
Outcome: Identifies at least ten lowercase letters out of order

Children can be heard singing an alphabet song or singing the alphabet letters in order, which leads some to say, "My child already knows the alphabet." Although this is a good start, it has little to do with the goal of identifying letters of the alphabet. An effective way to begin this task is to help children identify letters in their own names. Concentrate on letters in their names and in commonly seen environmental words such as *stop*, *go*, *push*, and *pull*.

Letter-of-the-week programs should be avoided. These have little meaning for children when used out of context.

Activities

Letters in Names

Have children begin to identify letters in names. As suggested in Lesson Activity 1, tape children's names to their workplaces. Have children see how many letters in their first and last names are also found in other children's names. Ask them to look for similar letters in and around the room and building. Later in the year, as suggested in the This Is My Work activity in Lesson Activity 2, have children begin writing their names (in any form) on their work.

Cut-and-Paste Names

Have children complete the Name Sheet provided in the appendix by cutting out the letters in their names and then pasting them in the appropriate spaces. You will need to reproduce extra letter sheets for this activity. Use the spaces available for longer names and the blank letter spaces where a letter is used more than one time. You might have children take this activity home so families can help with the process.

Month Names

Children can also begin to learn the letters in the names of the months. As they look at the calendar and count for the entire month, they can look to see what letters in the month correspond to the letters in their names. They can also match letters in their names to holiday names.

Name Bags

Make a name bag for each child using clear, sealable baggies. Use a marker to write each child's name on a bag, and then insert small papers with the individual letters inside. Sometimes as a group activity and more often as an individual activity, have the children take the letters out of the bags and match them to their names. Teach them to say the letters as they spell out their names.

Book Letter Search

Ask children to page through books to find any words that start with the same letter as their first name. Children can also search for words beginning with the same letter as their last name.

Letters, Letters, Everywhere

Add materials such as alphabet puzzles, magnetic letters, and foam letters to the classroom. Label shelves with words and pictures.

My Dog Bingo

Familiarize children with the song "B-I-N-G-O," found in the Music of Literacy section. Then, with the children, make up new names for the dog to insert into the song. See who has a dog, cat, or other pet with a five-letter name and sing that name in the song.

Checking Progress

Work with individual children on letter identification. Concentrate primarily on each child's first name. Use the individual assessment page to chart each child's progress.

Lesson Activity 11

Outcome: Recognizes and names a square, circle, rectangle, and triangle

Even though children have seen these basic shapes many times in their games, in their homes, as part of clothing patterns, and in book illustrations, many do not know the names of the shapes. Because the children do have the experience of seeing shapes in their world, they can easily accomplish this outcome during the program year.

Activities

Shapes Chart

Display a shape recognition chart. Many teachers make their own charts, but they also can be purchased from educational supply stores. The chart should serve as a reference point as children see these forms in other materials they examine, not for instructional drills and memorization. You can also use the chart during individual and group review when assessing children's progress in identifying shapes.

Environmental Shapes

Have children find shapes in the environment. Send a note home to families along with a sheet of paper that displays the four shapes. In the note, suggest ways for parents to explore the shapes with their children. For example, ask family members to assist children in identifying the shapes in their out-of-school environment, both inside and outside of the home. Encourage families to send in examples—such as written descriptions or photographs of shapes their child recognized in the environment—and set up a table in the classroom to display them. Use your classroom discussion time for individual children to describe their items to the class.

Shape Mobiles

Help the children construct shape mobiles. Because this activity may take place before children are skilled at cutting and pasting, it will require you to have the forms precut. Punch a hole at the top of each shape and, with a long piece of string, tie each shape to a spring. Display the mobiles in the classroom and, from time to time, use them in a review activity. Follow up with individual children who still need assistance. Send the mobiles home when most children can name all of the shapes.

Stringing Shapes

Encourage children to use the basic geometric forms in bead-stringing patterns. Have circles, triangles, rectangles, and squares available. Encourage children to vary the patterns to see which pattern has the most appealing look.

Shapes in Patterns

To reinforce the assessment activity on creating accurate patterns (see Shape Recognition and Copying assessment), work with individual children. Set up various patterns on a table using colors and shapes. Ask the children to duplicate each pattern and use the color and shape names when putting the pattern together.

Books about Shapes

Feature books that focus on shapes. Here are a few favorites of parents and teachers:

- *Brown Rabbit's Shape Book* by Alan Baker (2000). Bright and interesting pictures delight children, who will learn the basic shapes and some rather unusual ones as well!
- *The Wing on a Flea: A Book about Shapes* by Ed Emberley (2004). This rerelease of a 1960s classic still enchants with its vivid pictures and rollicking rhymes while helping children think about using shapes in art.
- *Shapes, Shapes, Shapes* by Tana Hoban (1997). A master of preschool concept books, Hoban does not disappoint with this bright photograph-based book.
- *When a Line Bends—A Shape Begins* by Rhonda Gowler Greene and James Kaczman (1999). Readers learn about ten different shapes and then begin to see them all around them.
- *A Triangle for Adaora: An African Book of Shapes* by Ifeoma Onyefulu (2000). Readers follow the photographs and storyline to find shapes while also learning about African culture.

Wallpaper Shapes

Borrow a wallpaper book from a local store, or ask for wallpaper samples the store might have on hand. With the children, go through the book or samples to find basic shapes used in the pattern. Select four different patterns for discussion and ask the children to select their favorites. Put the information on your data-collecting chart. (See Data-Collecting Activities in the Classroom Essentials section.) Discuss the reasons for their choices.

Taped Shapes

Tape shapes onto tops of tables so that you can easily refer to them when teachable moments occur.

Building with Shapes

During block play, discuss with the children why they use different shaped blocks in their structures (triangle for roof, rectangle for house and office buildings, and so on). Relate this to the discussion of the functions of shapes below.

Functions of Shapes

Discuss the functions of shapes—using a triangle for a tent, a circle for a wheel, squares and rectangles for storage boxes, and so on. Approach these discussions in a problem-solving mode. What would be the best shape for a tent? Why? For storage boxes? When might you use more than one shape for an item?

Shapes in Art

In the art center, have sheets of paper with basic shapes on them. Interested children can practice coloring, cutting, and pasting the shapes to make creative designs. Work with individual children who need assistance.

Lesson Activity 12

Outcome: Copies a square, circle, rectangle, and triangle

The successful achievement of the outcomes for Lesson Activities 11 through 14 is related to the development of small muscle control and proficiency in hand-eye coordination. Involve children in a host of classroom activities that help them increase dexterity. Puzzles, small block work, and bead stringing represent just a few of the daily activities that will help children develop manipulative skills. Learning to copy forms is enhanced when children can use their hands effectively. Help children learn how to hold crayons, pencils, and other writing tools correctly. Not all young children will do this naturally; be patient in helping them successfully control their hand movements.

Activities

Start by Tracing

Provide dot-to-dot outlines of the four shapes, and have children trace these forms on paper. Make copies of the Dot-to-Dot Shapes blackline master in the appendix and insert them into the transparent pocket folders described in the Name Folders activity in Lesson Activity 2. Also encourage the children to use different colored crayons and trace and overlap shapes of diferent sizes to make collages and designs.

Creative Use of Shapes

Involve children in activities that are related to duplicating forms. Have them draw their faces in different sizes on a sheet of paper. Encourage them to make animals with shapes or to draw other things in the world around them using shapes. (Caldecott winner Ed Emberley has a series of drawing books that might prove inspirational.) To help children practice the different components of shapes, construct dot-to-dot pictures for children to trace that include long straight lines, angles of different degrees, and curves. These dot-to-dot sheets are great for using in the transparent pocket folders described in the Name Folders activity in Lesson Activity 2.

Tools for Drawing Shapes

Provide tools that children can use when drawing shapes. Traditional tools such as rulers and compasses are helpful, as are objects such as lids or items with ninety degree corners that can be traced around.

Lesson Activity 13
Outcome: Identifies basic body parts

The terms *head, eyes, nose, ears, mouth, neck, arms, hands, body, legs, toes, feet,* and other nouns naming body parts may be words children have heard regularly at home. That does not mean they can associate those names with the representative body parts. Regular exposure to the identification of body parts over the years should provide children with the knowledge to identify each part of the body. Remember to be extremely sensitive during discussions around any children with special needs or challenges affecting their body parts.

Activities

Chart It
Post a teacher-made or store-bought body parts chart. Early in the year, ask the children to name the body parts as you point to them. This quick assessment lets you know how much instruction you need to provide.

Body Puzzle
Lay out a body parts floor puzzle for the children to work on. Allow this to be a choice activity during playtime. Use the puzzle yourself to help individual children increase their knowledge of body part names.

Doll Parts
After children have become more proficient at cutting and pasting, introduce them to the Fix the Doll blackline master provided in the appendix. Cut out the doll figure and the parts. Center the doll figure on a piece of paper and spread out the body parts. Show the children the picture of the doll that needs repair, and ask them what parts of the body need to be reattached. Ask the children to use the correct terms in their responses. Let the children help each other as needed. Note that there are several parts that do not fit. If someone suggests one of those parts, ask where it goes and then hold it up for them to see if it is correct. As the children mention appropriate parts, paste or glue the paper parts into place.

When you have completed the figure, tell the children you would like to have them show you how well they can repair their doll themselves. Post your completed figure where the children can use it as a model. Do not go through the activity with all the children one body part at a time; instead, the idea is to find out who has grasped the concept. Tell them to assemble all the parts in the right place before gluing them. Walk among the group, questioning individuals as you see the need. For example, ask the children "Is that where the part fits?" "Where do you think the hair belongs?" or "Does that part really fit?" When you see that individual children have assembled the figures correctly, they can go ahead and paste them to the paper. When all the children are done, review the parts of the body they have repaired. Review is essential because at this age children often lose the idea between introduction and involvement in the activity. The dolls can be displayed or taken home.

Here's My . . .

Have children regularly identify body parts on themselves, using a mirror for facial features. Using individual face photos, have the children identify those same features. Then, in a group activity, pair children and ask them to point to the other person's parts of the body as you name them.

Music for the Body

Several favorite songs use body parts and have children move them while singing. For example, in the Music of Literacy section, you can find the lyrics to "Head and Shoulders, Knees and Toes." Model how to act out the words of the song, touching each part in order. Have the children join in, and increase the pace with each repetition. You can also add or substitute other parts of the body. Another fun song included in the Music of Literacy section is "The Hokey Pokey." Enjoy moving your body parts along with the children!

Guess That Part

Play a guessing game in which you give clues and the children respond with the names of body parts. For example, you might say, "These help me run," or "These help me pick up things," or "These help me hear." At first, let children point to the parts. As the year progresses, expect them to verbally identify the parts.

Parts Art

Allow the children to make human figures out of modeling clay, snap-together blocks, and other three-dimensional materials in the art center.

Read about It

Find books in the library about body parts that you can read aloud and discuss with the children. One wonderful book to include in your room's literacy center is *Toes, Ears, and Nose! A Lift-the-Flap Book* by Marion Dane Bauer (2003). Readers can lift up flaps to see what body part is hidden under the clothing of a bundled-up baby.

Lesson Activity 14

*Outcome: Reproduces basic body parts
when drawing a person*

Knowing body parts and identifying them on a chart does not automatically translate into a child being able to draw a body with the appropriate parts in the correct places. It is the combination of this knowledge, a child's manipulative dexterity, and the ability to see the body in the mind's eye that provides children with the connections to draw a realistic reproduction of the body and its parts.

Activities

Establishing Level of Proficiency
Use the Reproducing Basic Body Parts assessment in the Periodic Assessment Tool to determine each child's ability to complete the task. Your findings should correspond with your observations during the My Teacher activity in Lesson Activity 2.

Life-Size Bodies
Early in the year, trace the children's bodies so they can see how unique they all are. Have each child lie face up on a large piece of butcher paper and then trace around the child's body with a marking pencil. With small groups, complete all of the tracing before having children move to the next step, which is filling in their body parts. With larger groups, do this activity over several days, letting the other children participate in choice time while you are doing the tracing. Using the body parts chart from Lesson Activity 13 as a reference, ask the children to fill in their main body parts. When this is completed, help each child identify her unique features—the color of his or her eyes, hair, skin, and clothes. Then let them finish coloring their project. Place the completed figures where there is room to put them side by side with their feet at the same level. This allows the children to compare each other by height and unique features such as color of hair and eyes. Ask families to send in a note stating any special attributes of their children. Read these to the children and attach each one to the corresponding figure. If families do not send a note, call them, write down their thoughts, and affix the slip in the same manner.

Checking Progress
To assess children's growing ability to correctly draw and place parts on the body, have them draw a person on a regular basis. Discuss children's

drawings by asking, "Where are the arms?" "Where are the legs?" and so on when parts have not been included. Then have children draw in the missing parts.

Bring in the News
Find articles and pictures in newspapers and magazines that offer opportunities for you to highlight body parts. You might also look for stories with photos that show people with prosthetics to use in a discussion about how people can compensate for the loss of limbs and other parts of the body. Of course, continue to be very sensitive to any special-needs children in your center.

Lesson Activity 15
Outcome: Demonstrates appropriate cutting skills

Many children at this age have had a variety of prior experiences using scissors, depending on the level of home or earlier program involvement. Still, all children need assistance learning to properly hold scissors, to turn the paper while cutting circles, and to cut square corners. The purpose of the cutting section of the Periodic Assessment Tool is to observe children's cutting skills without any instruction. Use this information to plan your instruction. There is every reason to initially involve the group in some cutting experiences prior to this instruction, however. This allows you to roam the room and take quick assessments of children's progress. Remember that this is a skill to develop and that the activities are not necessarily creative. The idea is to develop children's skills so they may be more adept in completing creative activities in the future.

Activities

Establishing Level of Proficiency
Conduct a pretest at the start of the year to determine each child's cutting proficiency. Without giving specific directions on how to cut and paste, demonstrate the assessment by cutting out the shapes from Shapes to Cut Out (provided in the appendix) and then pasting them on Shapes to Paste (provided in the appendix). Ask the children to do the same. As they work, observe them to determine their areas of difficulty in cutting. (You will focus on their pasting skills during Lesson Activity 16.) Record each child's level of proficiency on their assessment sheet.

Providing Direct Instruction
Based on the above assessment, provide additional cutting, pasting, tearing, and folding activities during group and self-directed learning times. Several cutting and folding activities are provided in the appendix. Direct instruction should include the following:

- Show the children that the efficient way to hold scissors involves the thumb and next two fingers. Purchase a demonstration pair of scissors with four holes for the teacher and the child to use as they cut together. Make sure there are also left-handed scissors available.
- Have children cut out around a shape from a larger sheet of paper. This makes cutting the actual form easier. Some teachers use the term "cutting it big."

- Demonstrate how to turn paper while cutting a curved line (rather than turning the scissors). This makes learning the skill easier.

Hand Tools

Assemble a group of everyday tools that require use of the hands, such as scissors, spring clothespins, tweezers, screwdrivers, pliers, tongs, and an assortment of clamps. Discuss why these tools are so important to us—they are extensions of our hands. Let some children hold ice cubes in their hands until their hands become too cold, then find a tool that makes holding the ice cube easier. Provide similar materials matched to tools for other tasks—cutting cloth rather than ripping it, turning screws with a screwdriver rather than with your fingers, or turning nuts with pliers rather than your hand—then discuss with the children that although these tools can do a better job than our hands, we still need to develop strength and agility in our hands in order to use the tools.

Fun with Folding

To develop the children's small muscles, have them practice folding paper. Demonstrate making simple paper-folding projects, such as a fan, a paper airplane, or a hat. Instructions for folding activities are provided in the appendix. Find books about origami in the library, and make them available during choice time. Also let children squeeze modeling clay and other malleable substances to help them build strength in their hands.

Cut This!

Provide different thicknesses of paper for children to use as they practice cutting. Cutting through thicker paper or multiple pages increases hand strength. Also have children cut out a variety of items from newspapers, magazines, and other print sources throughout the year.

Lesson Activity 16

Outcome: Demonstrates appropriate pasting skills

Children enter early childhood programs with some knowledge of how to paste or glue items together. This is a simple skill to teach, and most children will master it in a short time. Glue seems to have replaced paste in most early childhood rooms, so these terms can be used interchangeably.

Activities

Establishing Level of Proficiency

Administer the pretest described in Lesson Activity 15. (Use Shapes to Paste provided in the appendix.) As the children work, determine their level of pasting proficiency, and mark your findings on the assessment form. Problems tend to occur in two areas: (1) using too much glue for the item to be attached, or (2) putting glue on the background paper rather than the item to be affixed.

Providing Direct Instruction

Demonstrate to children that glue should only be put on the object being glued, not on the background paper. Begin by explaining that if they put the glue on the larger sheet, then they have to estimate the size of the item to be pasted. A well-done job should not have extra glue outside of the object itself, so it is better to put the glue on the object. Demonstrate putting an X in the middle of the piece to be pasted so that no glue is too close to the outside edges, then demonstrate how to "bunny hop" the glue by putting little dabs just inside the edge of the item to be pasted. Have the children try the procedure themselves. Help individual children as needed during this activity and throughout the program year. Update each child's assessment sheet periodically as they show progress.

Lesson Activity 17

Outcome: Understands the concept of print: Knows the difference between a letter, a word, and a sentence

Outcome: Understands the concept of print: Knows that print goes left to right and top to bottom with a return sweep

Outcome: Understands the concept of print: Knows that print tells the story and illustrations help tell the story

It is important to teach concepts of print through literature. This is in addition to daily reading of books for pure enjoyment, without asking questions or interrupting the story.

Children may have been read to by family members and caregivers since they were very young. Unless family members are versed in the process of teaching print awareness, however, these concepts are foreign to preschool children. An important part of learning to read is understanding these various concepts of print:

- A book is written by an author, who uses words to tell the story.
- A book is illustrated by an artist, who provides pictures to bring the story alive.
- A book has a front cover, back cover, and spine.
- A book has a title page.
- Print goes from left to right and top to bottom.
- Letters make up words, and words make up sentences.
- Quotation marks indicate that someone is talking.
- Books contain words, sentences, and paragraphs.
- Print uses a *?* to ask a question, a *.* to end a sentence, and an *!* to give emphasis to a part of the story.

You should not present all of the concepts of print on a daily basis. Instead, build different concepts of print into each day to help children eventually identify all of them.

Activities

Book Creators

Tell the children the name of the author and the name of the illustrator for every book read from the first day of the program. Show where these names are on the cover and on the title page of the book. As the weeks progress, occasionally ask the children what the author and illustrator contribute to the story.

Book Covers
Highlight the front and the back of each book. Lead the children to understand the purpose of the cover in protecting the book from damage and in providing the reader with the book title and a picture of something important in the story.

Letters and Words
Help children understand that letters make up words. Occasionally count the number of letters in the title, in the author's and illustrator's names, and in especially long words in the text.

Tracking Print
Periodically, use your finger to track the words as you read a book so that children begin to understand the concept of word. Read a short, familiar Big Book aloud and have individual children point to each word as the story goes along. Use this as an informal assessment to assist children in this learning.

Following the Flow
Use Big Books to demonstrate the flow of print. Use a pointer to show how print goes from left to right and top to bottom. Allow children to use their fingers or the pointer to show the direction that print flows as you read the story aloud. Over time, give all the children this opportunity.

What Is What?
Explain to children the difference between letters, words, sentences, and paragraphs. This can be done before or after a story is read. Periodically have the children point to a letter, a word, a sentence, and a paragraph to see if they can distinguish among the four.

Lesson Activity 18

*Outcome: Understands the concept of a story:
Knows that an author writes the story*

*Outcome: Understands the concept of a story:
Knows that an illustrator creates the pictures*

*Outcome: Understands the concept of a story: Knows
that a story has a beginning, a middle, and an end*

*Outcome: Understands the concept of a story:
Knows there are different characters in a story*

*Outcome: Understands the concept of a story:
Knows the story has a setting where it takes place*

*Outcome: Understands the concept of a story:
Knows that a conversation might take place*

Concepts of a story are new to preschool children. While each concept is found in most stories, children have not been exposed to the vocabulary of these concepts; therefore, the goal is to help children develop an understanding of the concepts of a story by the end of the preschool years.

Children enjoy listening to stories, and it is important to read to them for their enjoyment; however, it is also important that teachers periodically point out the concepts of a story so the children can incorporate these elements into their own stories, retell a story, or dramatize a story that has been read to them.

So, how can you accomplish the various types of activities suggested around story reading? Here is one plan: Read a story every day for a literary experience, and then alternate the post-story activities to include (a) initial sounds, (b) concepts of print, (c) concepts of a story, (d) retelling, and (e) predicting. Regular involvement with these concepts over the entire year will produce the desired outcomes.

Activities

Ask about Story Elements

As noted in previous lesson activities, read stories for a literary experience. However, when discussing the story afterward, you can model the vocabulary of the concepts of a story and story elements. For example, ask questions such as "Who are the characters in the story?" "Where does the story take place?" "What happened at the beginning of the story?" "What happened at the end?" (bring in the middle of the story as appropriate), "What was the problem the characters had?" or "How did they solve it?"

And Then What Happened?

After the children show an initial understanding of story concepts, review a story. Involve children by asking them to retell the various parts.

In My Story . . .

Have the children make up stories using the story concepts. Guide them by asking for ideas about characters and a story beginning, and then have them describe where the story takes place. Next, have the children add a middle part with a problem. Finally, ask them to brainstorm an ending.

Book Parts

Occasionally invite a child to show you the beginning of the book (the title page and first few pages), the middle of the book, and the end of the book (the last few pages). Choose different children to participate in this activity.

Change It Up

Have children think about different endings, a new setting, and the addition of new characters for their favorite stories.

What's Different?

Read different versions of folktales so children understand that characters and situations can be altered. For example, *Cinderella* exists in many cultures; *Little Red Riding Hood* has various endings; *Goldilocks and the Three Bears* features Goldilocks as a dog in one version, an old, silver-haired woman in another version, and a young, blond child in a third version.

Beginning, Middle, End

As the year progresses and children show growth in the outcomes, check their understanding of beginning, middle, and end of a story. We have provided a chart for this activity in the appendix. Begin by reading a short story to the class. Ask the children to talk about what happened in the first part of the story, what happened in the middle of the story, and what happened in the end of the story. Write those thoughts down on a large piece of paper. Then ask children to make simple drawings of the three parts of the story using the sheet provided in the appendix.

Lesson Activity 19

Outcome: Predicts what comes next in a story

Predicting is a comprehension strategy that all good readers and listeners use. It helps them understand and remember a story. When readers predict, they use clues from one part of the story to suggest what will happen next. In its most creative form, predicting allows children to think beyond the story. There are three different phases of predicting: (1) predicting the story line from looking at the book cover and a few of the pages, (2) predicting what will come next within the story, and (3) predicting what might happen after the story is concluded.

Activities

Predicting from the Cover and Introductory Pages

Begin reading sessions in the following way.

Teacher: "Today we are going to read _____. Look at the cover and tell me what you think this story will be about."

Accept all responses. Then turn to the inside of the book.

Teacher: "What do you think will happen? Let's look at the pictures to predict what will happen in the story."

From the children's responses, make a short language experience story.

Sam thinks _____ will happen.

Isabelle thinks _____ will happen.

Examine with the children which words are common. Be sure to talk with the children about their predictions to move them beyond guessing. Also help children understand that although pictures help to tell the story, the author uses words to actually tell the story.

Predicting What Will Happen Next in a Story

Early in the year, ask the children to predict the next sequence in a familiar story. While they will know the answer in their minds, this will require them to put their thoughts into words. Then ask children to predict the next sequence in an unfamiliar story.

Predicting After the Story Is Completed

At the end of the story, wonder aloud what might happen next: "What will the characters do? Where will they go next?" Ask children to respond to these questions.

Lesson Activity 20

Outcome: Retells a story with sufficient details

The retelling of stories by children develops recall and oral-language skills and is an excellent way to check children's comprehension. These are critical factors in children's later reading experiences. Developing these skills in the early years gives children a head start in becoming accomplished readers.

In the beginning of the year, read stories for children's enjoyment and to expand their awareness of the variety of stories and books. To assess their understanding of the story, have them do simple retelling. This can be done as a group and individually. A typical retelling activity might look like this:

> Read the story with no interruptions so the children hear the flow of the entire story. When the story has ended, ask the group to retell the story in their own words. After they retell it, ask for more details until you have a fairly complete retelling.

Activities

Add the Concepts of a Story

Regularly continue the retelling process described above and also begin to include the concepts of a story. You might ask questions, such as "Who can tell us what happened first?" "What happened second?" and "How did the story end?" Let other children add to the recollections of their classmates.

Make Changes

Encourage children to retell a story using a different ending, a different setting, or different characters. Also have fun with the children by making up a different version of a folktale. For example, rather than a gingerbread character rolling away, being chased by different characters, and finally eaten by a fox, it might be a pizza character that rolled out of a restaurant, chased by appropriate characters, and finally eaten for lunch in the preschool.

Act It Out

The ability to retell also can be demonstrated through dramatizations of stories. Create storytelling boxes with simple props for familiar and new stories. The dramatizations do not have to be formal affairs in front of live audiences. Suggest that the children retell stories to their dolls or to their classmates as they play in the various centers such as the housekeeping or dress-up center.

Flannelboards
Provide simple flannelboard pieces to accompany often-read stories. Let children use these as they retell stories.

Now Hear This
Make recordings of children retelling a story. Hearing themselves as story-tellers is a thrill, and they will want to share the tapes, CDs, or MP3s with their family members. Of course, you should encourage students to retell stories they hear at school to their parents throughout the year.

Lesson Activity 21

Outcome: Differentiates and reproduces rhyming sounds

Learning to rhyme words is not only an enjoyable experience for young children, but this phonological awareness skill has been shown to be a significant predictor of successful reading achievement in later school years. However, rhyming is not always an easy activity for young children to master. When helping children learn the concept of rhyme, understand that they can use real words or nonsense words to accomplish the task.

Activities

Rhyming Names
Have children produce real or nonsense words that rhyme with their first and last names (for example, *Jacob, macob, bacob; Jim, slim, him; Carla, Marla, Darla; John, Juan, lawn*).

My Rhymes
Play a game in which you say a word and the children repeat it and add a word that rhymes. Help children who are having problems with the rhyming sound, and allow children to help each other. Work independently with children who are struggling.

Rhymes in Literature
Read books by authors who use rhyming words, such as those by Dr. Seuss or books of Mother Goose rhymes. As children become familiar with these books, have them periodically add the last rhyming words. You can also use standard fingerplays that feature rhyming words, such as "Itsy, Bitsy Spider" (found in the Music of Literacy section).

Idiomatic Rhymes
Introduce children to common phrases that have rhyming words. Some examples include *willy-nilly, brain drain, lucky ducky,* and so on.

Musical Rhymes
Sing rhyming songs (for example, "Hush, Little Baby," which is featured in the Music of Literacy section.) As children become familiar with the songs, have them change or extend the lyrics with different rhyming words.

Same Yet Different?
Have children think of words that rhyme. Write down the words so that children see that at times the same sound can be written in different ways; for example, *seat/feet, bird/heard, spy/eye.*

Lesson Activity 22

Outcome: Differentiates and reproduces beginning sounds

Identifying and reproducing beginning sounds is a new experience for preschool children. Learning beginning sounds is a subtle skill. Avoid teaching beginning sounds in isolation. It is not "*B* as in /b/." It is "*B* as in *book*." Introducing beginning sounds this way provides an accurate relationship between sounds and letters. Even though the assessment for this skill is a midyear activity, start the process early in the year so that children have an awareness of the concept when the assessment takes place. Accomplishing this outcome will occur across the preschool years. Incorporate this outcome into many enjoyable activities while also concentrating on the following ideas.

Activities

Story Words

Story time is one of the most effective times to involve children because it provides authentic experiences in learning beginning sounds. Select a story (Big Books work especially well) and a word within the story that begins with the same letter as the name of a child in your class. (For example, if you have a student named Devon, you might select the word *dog*.) You will also want to have the name chart handy that you created for Lesson Activity 1.

Begin by reading the story from start to finish. Then turn the children's attention to the word that you have previously selected. Say, "I see a word in the story that I really like. I see the word *dog*." Point to the word on the page, and write it where the children can see it. Ask, "Can you think of another word that begins with that same sound?" Accept children's correct ideas, and question those who aren't correct by redirecting them to produce the beginning sound.

Then ask if anyone has a name that starts with the target sound. Invite the children to look for a word (or words) on the name chart that starts with the same sound as *dog*. Help them find, for example, Devon's name. You might select another word during the same activity, using another child's name. Don't make this a daily activity, but do it often during the first three months of the program to help children understand this concept. Initially, young children frequently confuse this activity with rhyming and will respond to your question with a rhyming word. Redirect their responses to the beginning sound.

Name Sounds

Periodically, have children think of words that start with the same beginning sound as their first name. You can also focus on last names. At times, identify the names of two or more children that start with the same beginning sound. When you work with the calendar, you can have children identify classmates' first and last names that begin the same as the name for a day of the week or month.

Picture Sort

Have children sort pictures of items according to the beginning sounds of the objects' names.

Lesson Activity 23

*Outcome: Shows growth in writing alphabet
and picture code systems*

Writing involves the integrated use of small-motor skills, visual perception, and hand-eye coordination. From birth, and prior to age three, children are involved in various scribble stages. At age three, they begin a phase called *named scribbling*. Typically they ask, "What did I draw?" and can produce a specific letter on request. Children at this stage may demonstrate pretend writing as they are at work in various play centers. At age four, children can write a version of their name and begin the progress to readable writing. Picture writing, or drawing, will be a sign that children can depict an idea in print. This stage is followed by writing the alphabet, where letter symbols represent the sounds of language.

The preschool years include important milestones in the development of writing. Because of the wide range of individual differences at this initial stage of writing, you need to be aware of each child's present stage and then find the balance between accepting that current level and giving guidance to help them to the next level. The key is to involve children in the variety of writing stages so they experience success and growth during this time.

Journal writing is a very important strategy for achieving this outcome. You will find a special journaling section following Lesson Activity 28.

Activities

Where to Begin
A good starting point for writing is the picture drawing of the My Teacher activity described in Lesson Activity 2. Continue by having children write their names as described in that lesson. Later, children can write environmental print words.

We Write a Lot!
Collect from families the various kinds of writing found in the home, such as envelopes from letters received in the mail, grocery lists, handwritten recipes, e-mail, and other examples, to enable children to see the important role writing plays in their lives.

Writing Center

Set up a writing center or writing table to encourage individual writing. Consider including the following items:

- a wide variety of paper styles, sizes, and shapes
- chalkboards and magic slates
- an easel and a whiteboard
- many types of marking tools, such as pencils, crayons, paintbrushes, and markers
- an old typewriter
- a computer
- alphabet charts
- rulers
- rubber alphabet stamps
- staplers
- paper punches
- scissors
- yarn and bread ties
- paper fasteners

All of these items do not need to be available all the time. Changing materials keeps the center interesting for the children. For example, putting out small green paper in March after reading a book about leprechauns can lead to note writing in the classroom. In February, heart-shaped paper can spark the idea of writing Valentine cards to each other. New materials and modeling by the teacher can make this a favorite center in the classroom.

Writing at Centers

Highlight writing opportunities in all centers. For example, provide pencil and paper to take orders or record messages in the restaurant, grocery-store, flower-shop, housekeeping, and shoe-shop centers. Encourage children to leave notes for others when they want play materials left intact for the next day.

Signing In

As children become adept at checking in with check-in sticks (see Individual Attendance Devices in the Classroom Essentials section), change the roll-call activity. Provide a large laminated sheet of paper with children's photos and names, and have them sign in with their signatures.

My Storybook

Encourage children showing proficiency in writing to write and illustrate their own stories. Assemble and bind the final products. Have children read their stories to the class, and then put them in the library center for others to look at.

Artwork Titles

Have children title any pictures they draw. Write down what they tell you so the titles can be shared with others. Display the children's choice of pictures in the classroom for several weeks. This is especially appropriate if you have been involving the children in visits to museums or have featured an artist-of-the-month where you have dealt with the titles of artwork.

Take-Home Journals

Initiate an activity where children can take a doll or a stuffed animal home for the evening. Include a journal in the take-home bag. Encourage family members to jot down notes about interesting happenings. The next day, read the journal entry to the children for their enjoyment and to show the value of writing in recalling the experience.

Children's Journals

Use journals to promote writing. Provide simple books with unlined paper that children can use to record pictures, words, and experiences. Pages from the journals make wonderful work samples, revealing for families their children's growth in writing. We have provided detailed information about journal writing after Lesson Activity 28, including

- three steps for making journal writing successful;
- ground rules for journal writing;
- a description of the teacher's role during journal writing.

Birthday Cards

Set up a birthday-card center. Send a note home asking for the birthdays of family members. On the day of a family member's birthday, meet with individual children and help each one construct an easy four-fold card with a drawing of their choice on the front cover. Have them dictate a simple birthday greeting to include in the card. On the inside left of the card, write the child's message for the recipient. Initially, encourage the children to sign the card on the inside right at their level of writing. As the year progresses, have them copy the simple greeting on the right side of the card.

Lesson Activity 24

Outcome: Reads simple stories using pictures and/or words

As the year progresses children will begin to read simple messages and stories. Picture reading will be the easiest, but eventually children will be able to read combinations of pictures and alphabet. Because various code systems play an important role in all aspects of our society, exposing children to a wide variety of them provides useful activities and an awareness of the role of code systems in their lives.

Activities

My Story

Have children represent ideas and stories through drawings and/or dictation. Ask them to read their stories back to you and their classmates.

Repeated Lines

Ask children to read the common word lines in repetitive stories, for example, "Brown Bear, Brown Bear, what do you see?"

Letters

Have children dictate and illustrate a letter and then send it to someone they know (a friend, grandparents, and so on). You might also have children dictate a letter to themselves, fold it and place it in an envelope, add the address, stamp it, and mail it. Wait for the return mail and point out all the markings on the envelope. Ask the children if they remember what they wrote, then read the letter to them.

Rebus Work

Provide simple rebus items—sentences constructed of print and pictures—for children to read. For example, you can make up rebus directional signs, such as "Go (green on a stoplight) to the store (picture of a food store)." Help children learn the sight words used in connecting the graphics—in this case, the words *to* and *the*. You can also use the rebus approach to write a daily message to the children, for example, "I am *happy* (happy face) to see you."

Language Experience Stories

Review the guidelines for Language Experience Stories in the Classroom Essentials section, and plan to work with the children on writing language experience stories after any number of experiences. Examples include a field trip, a visit by a resource person, viewing a film or a video, or any other event. An appropriate format for a language experience story follows:

> Our Zoo Visit
> Alex said, "I liked the alligator."
> Joseph said, "The monkeys were funny."
> Colleen said, "I had fun."
> Josie said, "I liked the bus ride."

It's important that you write quickly and include no more than four or five quotes per story. If it takes too long to do the activity, young children will lose interest and be unable to recall what they said. Photographs can be added to aid the children as they read their story.

After a story is written, have the children read what they said. Point out similar words, question marks, and so on, and have all the children read the story as you track the print with your hand or a pointer.

Keep the language experience stories available so the children can continue to read them in the following days and weeks.

Photo Language Experience Story

Create a photo language experience story. Take photos at important junctures of a field trip. Print the photos, then begin the activity by having the children identify which part of the trip each photo represents: getting into the van/bus, stopping at the bakery, looking at the display, meeting the baker, watching the baker ice a cake, eating the cake, and riding the bus back to the preschool. Display the photos in random order during this part of the activity.

Next, ask the children to help you sequence the photos to show the order in which the events happened. Temporarily assemble them in order on an easel or board. Later, paste them on a large piece of paper in order of the trip, from left to right. Write words that describe each photo. Display the photo story, and have the children narrate the sequence. Do this over several days with the group. Some children will ask to show you what they know. Some children will need help reading the pictures or words.

Lesson Activity 25

Outcome: Shows growth in vocabulary and language use

Children at this age enter school with a variety of language backgrounds. This is especially true with the increased number of nonnative speakers in preschool settings. The teachers and the program can have a tremendous impact on children's vocabulary development and language use. To effectively communicate with others, children need to increase their vocabulary and improve their language use.

Activities

Let's Talk about It
Engage in frequent one-on-one conversations with children.

Let's Experience It
Provide children with many firsthand experiences. Read articles related to the topic under study, invite resource people into the classroom, and go on field trips. Help children find the words to describe what they are doing, hearing, and seeing.

Expand Vocabulary
Introduce new words in stories and in topics under study.

Talk about News
Display a news bulletin board. (See News Bulletin Boards in the Classroom Essentials section.) Bring in stories related to the children's lives for discussion.

Question It
Discuss what a question is. Help children learn how to ask direct questions to gather information.

Describe It
Have children use descriptive language when retelling a story they have heard or when telling a story of their own. Similarly, ask for more details when children describe experiences they have had.

What Did You Say?
Work with children on speaking clearly and loudly enough to be heard in both small and large groups.

Manners

Teach children to use common social conventions, especially those focused on words such as *excuse me, please, and thank you.*

Telephone Game

Help children learn how to relay messages accurately. Play a game where the teacher tells the first child something of interest and each person passes it along until the last person tells what he heard. Talk about the importance of passing messages accurately in home and school situations.

ELL Tips

For non-English speaking young children, make a set of picture/word cards showing common places within your program, such as the bathroom, the large activity room, the music room, the outside playground, and other important places. From the first day of class, use these cards in conjunction with verbal directions. For example, show the card of the playground as you say, "Now we will get ready to play in the playground." The non-English speaking children can see where they are going and quickly make that word a part of their vocabulary. This builds vocabulary and makes them immediately successful in getting to places in and around the building.

Spoken Directions

Give children two and three step directions. For example, you could say "Go wash your hands and sit down at the table. Then get out your red crayon."

Lesson Activity 26

*Outcome: Identifies common words found
inside and outside the classroom*

Children begin to recognize words before they realize that words are made up of letters. For example, they can recognize the words *stop, gas, exit,* and common store and restaurant names without knowing the letters in the words. They are, in essence, reading the word code. Taking advantage of this kind of learning, use common words children see in the environment every day even though they are not necessarily looking for those words. By having them read the symbols, you help children translate them into the words they represent.

Activities

Words on Signs

Start by identifying words on signs around the room and building, such as *exit, boys, girls, men, women, office, director,* and *lunchroom.* Explain why these are important words to know. Then play a solve-the-problem game by asking questions, such as "What word would help if you were in a building in which there was a fire?" or "What words would help if you had to go to the bathroom?"

Words on Labels

Expand awareness of words to include the labels found in the room. It is helpful to put pictures corresponding to words in centers so all of the children can read the signs using different code clues. For example, include drawings or photos of blocks by the block area, puzzles by the puzzle area, and so forth.

Words on Bulletin Boards

Using titles on bulletin boards will help children recognize words that describe their work. For example, you might title a bulletin board, "Our Yarn and Glue Pictures."

Words, Words, Everywhere

Look for common words on field trips. To reinforce their knowledge of words, bring in advertisements of area stores, restaurants, and places that children and their families frequent. As children come to recognize words, add each new word to a word wall in your classroom. Read the words on the word wall with the entire group from time to time.

Lesson Activity 27

Outcome: Understands and uses comparative terms

Many children enter preschool programs with a practical understanding of a few comparative terms. For example, they can quite easily identify the largest dessert when faced with two cookies or two ice-cream cones. They might know they are taller than their younger brother or sister. They are not familiar with the many comparative terms that are frequently used, however, including words that describe positions. Model these words as you use them in many opportunities throughout each day. Regularly set up some activities to help children understand and identify how these terms are used in many situations in their lives.

COMPARATIVE WORDS	POSITIONAL WORDS
taller, tallest	over, under
longer, longest	above, below
harder, hardest	in front of, in back of
softer, softest	beside, between
larger, largest	inside, outside
smaller, smallest	up, down
lighter, lightest	top, bottom
heavier, heaviest	nearer, farther
easier, easiest	

Activities

Up, Down, All Around

Regularly use positional words as they apply to various activities in the daily schedule. Say things such as "Raise your hands *up*," "Put them back *down*," "Stand *behind* your partner," and "Stand *in front of* your partner." The number of opportunities to use these terms is unlimited.

Hard and Soft

Help children understand the use of words like *harder/hardest* and *softer/ softest*. Provide them with three or four balls of various firmnesses, including a spongy ball. Pass two balls around and ask which is *harder* and which is *softer*. Keep interchanging the balls and adding a third into the mix until children see that the word ending -*est* is a relative, or comparative, term used for describing more than two items. Sometimes an item is *harder* than one item, but when compared to two or more items it may be the *hardest*.

What's Easiest?

Use a group activity to demonstrate this concept. Ask children which is the easiest for them to do: hop on one foot, walk on a balance beam, or do a somersault. Graph the children's responses. Discuss how these terms may apply differently to different children depending on the task. Add more tasks and switch back and forth from comparing two to comparing more than two, to gain a greater understanding of the terms. You can also complete the charting activity for other terms, such as *tastiest* or *funniest*.

Lesson Activity 28

Outcome: Shows initiative in engaging in simple reading and writing activities

Children need to understand that they are involved in reading and writing many times during the program. Most of the time it will involve pictures. Sometimes it will involve words. At other times, children will be dealing with symbols, such as an arrow pointing in a certain direction. Reinforce to children that they are at the beginning stages of reading and writing and will be progressing to higher levels throughout the year. This puts the process of learning to read and write in a positive light, rather than giving children the mistaken notion that they are not reading or writing until they have learned the alphabet and can read and write words.

Activities

This outcome is the culmination of all of the lesson activities included in this book. If those activities are used on a regular basis, in both group and individual formats, and adjusted to the level of each child in the program, tremendous progress will be made toward helping all children be better prepared for the next level of education and to better interact with their daily environment. The Periodic Assessment Tool will then become the measure of the success of this program. The variations in individual growth should be minimized if you have been working with individual children and reinforcing areas of needed growth throughout the year.

Journal Writing

Three Steps for Success

Step 1: Properly Introduce the Journal and Journal Writing

Begin by introducing the children to their blank journals sometime during the second month of school. By this time, the children should have an understanding of the routines and rituals of the classroom. Children might have their first experience with their journals with the creation of a self-portrait and a name-writing sample for the cover. Ownership of the journal is important if the children are to see their writing as meaningful and authentic.

Step 2: Provide a Journal for Each Child

Individual journals can be made from three-ring binders or unlined pads of paper. They also can be constructed daily by stapling a new journal page onto those from previous days. Some teachers use plain white typing paper stapled at the left side. Other teachers provide bound books with many pages. Still others use three-ring binders with three-hole punched paper. Whatever form the journal takes, the important thing is that each child is able to recognize her own name so all of the children can retrieve their journals from storage and feel a sense of ownership of them.

Step 3: Provide Time for Journaling

Journal writing can be done at several times during the day. While it can be done at times as a group activity, it is best not to have a set amount of minutes when everyone must write. The range of writing is so great at this age; some children will write for fifteen minutes while others will just make a few marks and be done. Finding the best time in the daily schedule should be based on your understanding of the developmental levels of the children you are working with.

Many teachers schedule a journaling time right before free play so that children can write in their journals for as long as they wish. It is important that when children are finished with their writing, they show it to someone while their ideas are still fresh. This means that at least one adult should be sitting near the children while they write. As children become more independent with their journals, they will use them for longer periods of time and begin to share what they have written with one another.

Journals also can be introduced as a free-time opportunity for three- and four-year-olds. Simply include the writing center or writing table as an option during that time.

Ground Rules

Once the children know what their own journals look like and where they are to be stored for the year, the ground rules can be introduced.

Begin as a Class

First, model how you would write in your own journal (which should look exactly like the children's). It works well to clip the open journal to an easel so the children can watch as you write. Begin your own journal by recording the date at the top of the page and saying the words you are writing and the individual letters as you write them. For example, if the journals were started on October 15, you would say, "October fifteenth, (and the year)." As you write, you would say, "O-C-T-O-B-E-R fifteenth, two thousand . . ."

Model an Entry

Once the date is recorded, it is time to record one or two simple sentences. Model how you might select an idea from your own life or a school activity, talk about the idea, organize your thoughts aloud with the children, and then draw a picture and write about the idea. You should model the concept of spelling things the way they sound (sound spelling).

You should also share the Stages of Writing chart (provided in the appendix) with the children, being sure to call each of the stages *real writing*. You can share a variety of samples of children's writing done in previous years. At every writing stage, it is important for children to feel that their writing is legitimate writing.

Once you have modeled writing a page or two in your journal, reread your writing to the group. When the journal is reread aloud, track the print with an index finger.

Set the Parameters

You also need to set the parameters for journal writing:

- The journal belongs to the child.
- The journal contains ideas that the writer wishes to add to the journal.
- Others may write in someone's journal only if the owner requests it or gives permission. This includes what you might add to the journal as they write, single words for the child to copy, or when taking dictation.

You should then give the children some procedures for what to do with the journal when the writing is complete. Here are some possible ideas:

- Read your journal to a teacher.
- Read your journal to a friend.

- Ask a teacher to help you write more in your journal.
- Ask a friend to add to your journal.
- Sign up for a turn in the author's chair to read your journal at the end of the day.
- Put your journal back in its storage place when you have finished sharing it.

The Teacher's Role during Journal Time

Your role is an important factor in children's growth in writing. The wide range of individual differences requires varied approaches to foster each child's writing ability. The most important role, however, is to clearly communicate to each child and to the class that there are many levels of acceptable writing that they will see and use during the year, and that each level is valued and legitimate.

During the time that children are writing in their journals, you can do several specific things:

- Be available to encourage the children who are having difficulty thinking of an idea or topic to write about.
- When asked how to spell a word, encourage the child to spell it the way he thinks it sounds. You may refer the child to words on the word wall in the classroom. Sometimes you can write a word on a card or slip of paper for the child to copy. Sometimes you can simply spell a word correctly for children who have demonstrated a willingness to take risks with their writing.

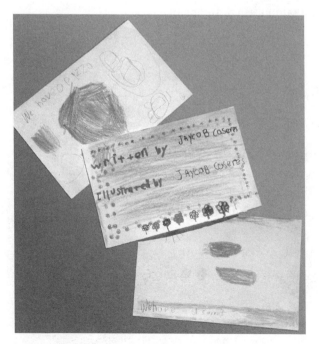

- Be available to listen when children read from their journal pages and encourage children to read their journals to one another.
- Encourage some children to put their journals in a read-to-me box by the author's chair to be read at the end of the day. When encouraging the children who read at the end of the day, it is important for you to remember to encourage all levels of readers and writers, rather than only those children who have progressed the furthest in their writing development. It is best to have no more than three readers at the end of the day. Give all of the children the opportunity over the next few days.

PART SIX

Appendix

6

Appendix

Blackline Masters

Tips for Families to Encourage Positive Reading Behaviors

Family Letter

Name Sheet (Lesson Activity 10)

Dot-to-Dot Shapes (Lesson Activity 12)

Fix the Doll (Lesson Activity 13)

Shapes to Cut Out (Lesson Activity 15)

Cutting Lines (Lesson Activity 15)

Cutting a Spiral (Lesson Activity 15)

Folding a Hat (Lesson Activity 15)

Folding a Cup (Lesson Activity 15)

Shapes to Paste (Lesson Activity 16)

Beginning, Middle, End (Lesson Activity 18)

Stages of Writing (Journal Writing)

Milestones for Three- and Four-Year-Olds

I'll Wait Timeline

Tips for Families to Encourage Positive Reading Behaviors

When your home is full of reading experiences, your child will benefit! For example, when you read aloud often to your child, she will

- develop oral vocabulary;
- develop reading concepts;
- have a good foundation for writing and spelling;
- be much more likely to have successful reading achievement in future school reading programs.

Other things you can do to build a rich reading environment include the following:

- Read yourself, and be sure that your child sees you reading. Occasionally point out something to your child that you have read in the newspaper, a magazine, or mail you receive.
- Read a story to your child every day. Make sure all of the readers in your household take a turn.
- Find a comfortable spot for reading with your child during the day. The bed is fine for evenings!
- View reading as a positive activity. Never threaten that you will not read a story if a child misbehaves. Instead, reward your child by reading an extra book at bedtime. With older children, be consistent in their bedtimes, but allow them to read an extra half hour once they are in bed.
- Take books along whenever you leave home, whether it's to take a trip, to go to the store, or to visit with friends.
- Provide paper and crayons for your child to draw a favorite book character. Accept scribbles at first. Help your child write the character's name on the drawing. Find a place to display these treasures!
- Register for a public library card and regularly let your child select books to borrow. Look for library story times to enjoy when your family schedule permits.
- Read a variety of storybooks, poetry books, and information books with your child.
- Select books that relate to the experiences and interests of your child (camping, sports, animals, and so on).
- If you have the equipment, audiotape yourself reading favorite selections so that your child can listen to the stories by himself or herself.

- Talk about books you enjoyed as a child and why you liked them so much. If they are still available in the library, share them with your child.
- Help your child talk with grandparents or neighbors to see what their favorite books were when they were children. Again, see if these books are still available in the library.
- Talk about books you are currently reading yourself—things the characters do and events that happen—or select one funny passage to share with your child.
- Purchase books for your child as holiday and birthday gifts.
- Point out useful words in your home and neighborhood, such as *exit, school crossing, walk, don't walk, stop,* and others.

Activities to Do When Reading Books to Your Child

- Before reading a story, have your child "read the illustrations" to predict what the story might be about. Accept simple thoughts at first, but then urge your child to expand on the ideas as he grows older.
- After reading a book, have your child identify a favorite character or part of the book. Ask him or her to explain why the character or event is so special.
- Read books with rhyming words and repeated phrases. Invite your child to fill in ending rhymes or to join in on reading the refrains or repeated story lines.
- Occasionally point to each word as you read to show that reading goes from left to right and top to bottom. This also helps your child understand the concept of a word.
- Occasionally ask your child to retell a story in her own words. Be content with simple thoughts at first, but prod for longer responses over the years. Having simple puppets available may encourage your child to retell the story through the characters.
- Ask your child to predict what will happen next in a story or after the story is completed. This is not an easy task for some children. Provide enough time for your child to think of some possibilities. When asking your child to predict what might happen next in a story, point to various pictures and talk about what the characters are like to provide clues. When asking your child to predict what might happen after a story ends, share some ideas you have as a model.
- Make reading a joyful experience by always showing your own enthusiasm.

Dear Families,

We are pleased that you have enrolled your child in our program. Thank you! We believe that early childhood programs are enhanced by parent involvement, and we encourage you to share your hobbies, collections, occupations, and skills with all of the children in our program.

It would be helpful to us, as we plan this year's program, to have the following information about each child's adult family members.

Name _____ Telephone number_____

1. Do you play a musical instrument?   Yes ☐ No ☐

If yes, please tell us about it and whether or not you would be willing to share your talent with the children. _____

_____

2. Do you have a collection that you are willing to share?   Yes ☐ No ☐

If yes, please tell us about the collection. _____

_____

3. Which of your interests or hobbies might you like to tell the children about?

_____

4. Would you be willing to talk about your job with the children?   Yes ☐ No ☐

If yes, please tell us about the work you do. _____

_____

_____

_____

5. Do you have a "green thumb" to help us with planting?   Yes ☐ No ☐

6. Do you sew?   Yes ☐ No ☐

7. Can you repair broken toys and games?   Yes ☐ No ☐

8. Would you like to come to the classroom occasionally to read
to or work with children in small groups?   Yes ☐ No ☐

9. What are the best days and times of the day that you would be available to share your skills and interests with the children? _____

10. Do you need transportation to and from the program?   Yes ☐ No ☐

Thank you for your willingness to share yourself with the children. Your experiences add a unique personal touch to our program. By watching you share, your child experiences the joy of seeing you as a part of their education.

Please return this form within the next few days.

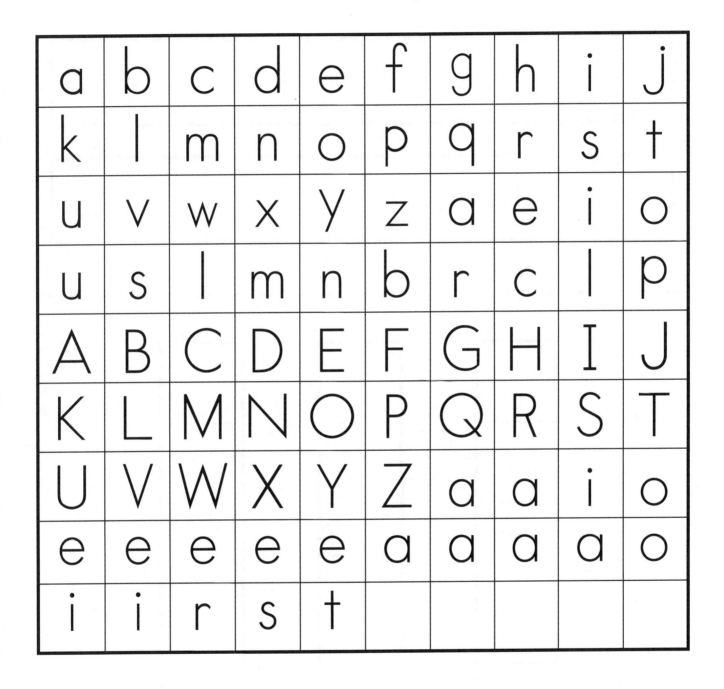

a	b	c	d	e	f	g	h	i	j
k	l	m	n	o	p	q	r	s	t
u	v	w	x	y	z	a	e	i	o
u	s	l	m	n	b	r	c	l	p
A	B	C	D	E	F	G	H	I	J
K	L	M	N	O	P	Q	R	S	T
U	V	W	X	Y	Z	a	a	i	o
e	e	e	e	e	e	a	a	a	a	o
i	i	r	s	t					

My Name

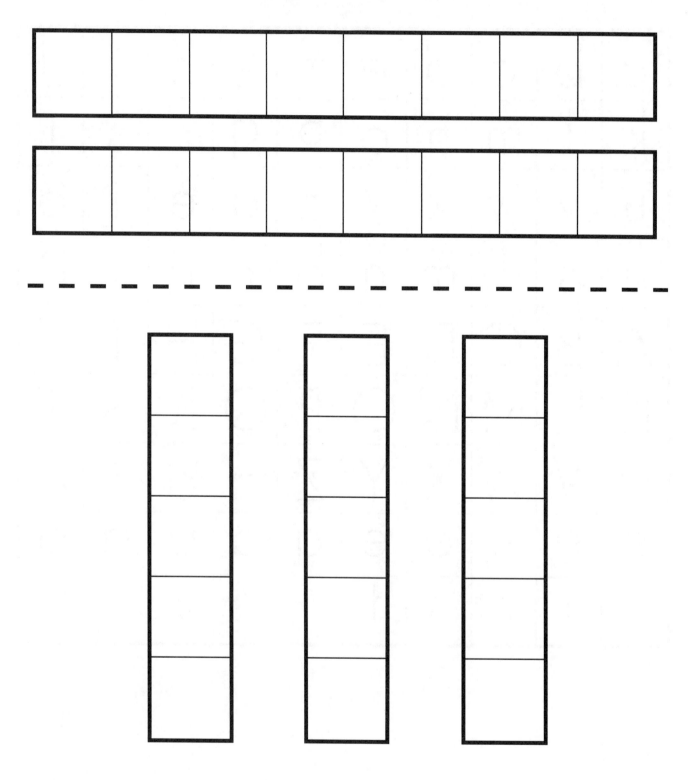

Dot-to-Dot Shapes (Lesson Activity 12)

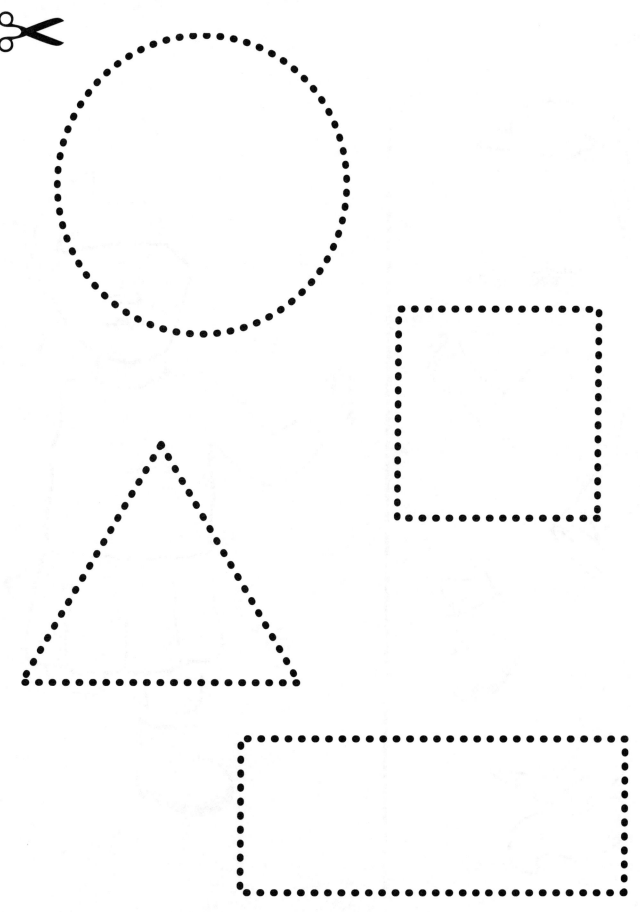

Fix the Doll (Lesson Activity 13)

Shapes to Cut Out (Lesson Activity 15)

Have children use scissors to practice cutting the different shapes.

Cutting Lines (Lesson Activity 15)

Have children use scissors to practice cutting along the different types of lines.

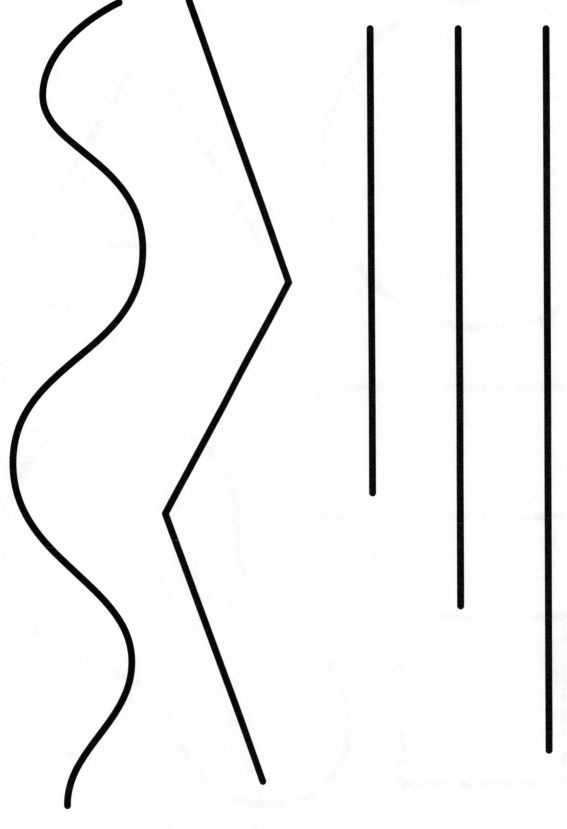

Cutting a Spiral (Lesson Activity 15)

Have children use scissors to cut the spiral, beginning on the outside edge.

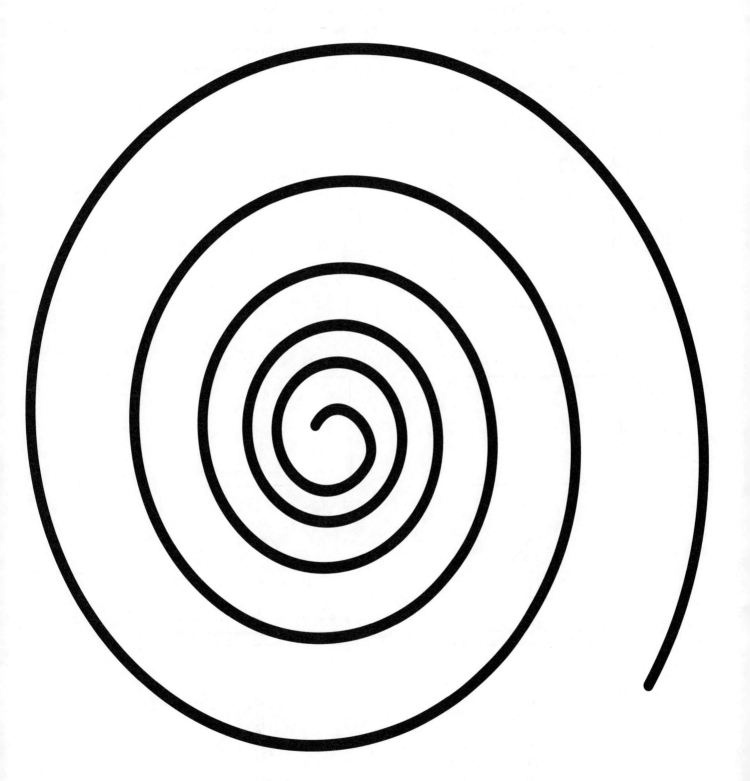

Folding a Hat (Lesson Activity 15)

If necessary, give these oral directions for each step of the folding process.

Fold a sheet of paper in half.
Fold it in half again, then open it.
Fold the upper-right corner down,
   to the center fold.

Repeat with the left corner.
Fold the outer bottom strip up.
Fold the other bottom strip back.
Press all the folds and open the hat!

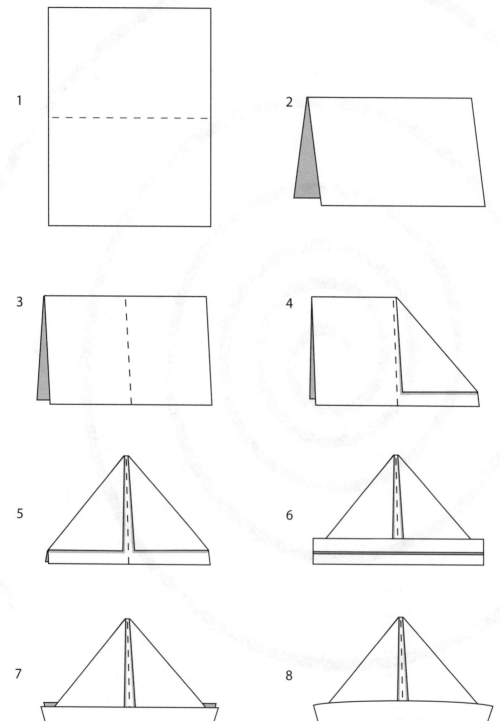

Folding a Cup (Lesson Activity 15)

If necessary, give these oral directions for each step of the folding process.

Fold a square of paper to make a triangle.
Place the triangle with the folded side down.
Fold the bottom-left corner up.
Repeat with the bottom-right corner.

Fold the outer triangle at the top down.
Fold the other triangle at the top back.
Press all the folds and open the cup.

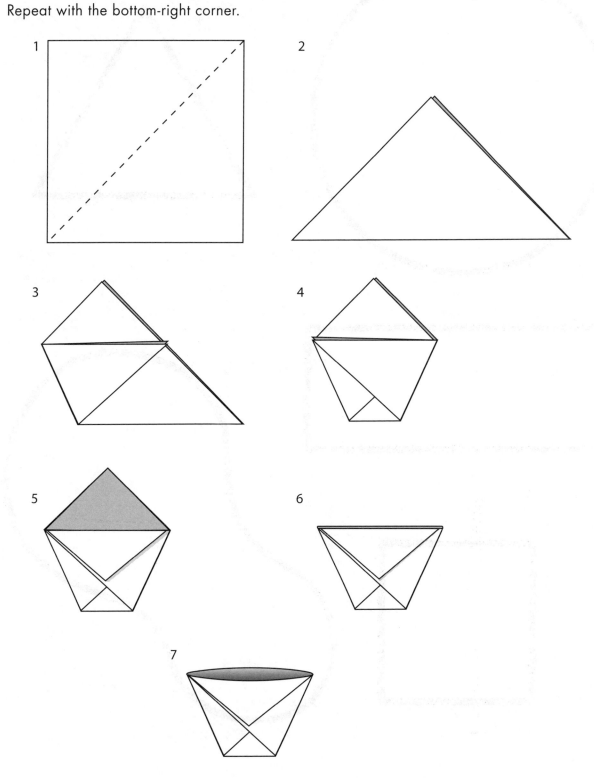

Shapes to Paste (Lesson Activity 16)

Beginning, Middle, End (Lesson Activity 18)

BEGINNING	MIDDLE	END

Stages of Writing (Journal writing)

Shown here are the stages through which you can expect children to move as they learn to write.

Stage 1: Scribbles (created by spontaneous movement)
Stage 2: Shapes (more planned)
Stage 3: Groupings (shapes are put together in a deliberate way)
Stage 4: Pictures (representational drawings)
Stage 5: Alphabet (writing letters)
Stage 6: Doodles (deliberate designs made from controlled scribbling)

Milestones for Three- and Four-Year-Olds

Name: _____

Age: _____

Teacher: _____

Emotional Development	Not Yet	Sometimes	Frequently	Almost Always
Demonstrates competency in recognizing and describing own emotions				
Uses words instead of actions to express emotions				
Shows empathy and caring for others; e.g., gives comfort to a child who has fallen, accepts disabilities and diversity				
Shows self-control in appropriately handling emotions				

Social Development	Not Yet	Sometimes	Frequently	Almost Always
Understands others' rights				
Cooperates; helps and shares with others				
Uses words to resolve conflicts peacefully; e.g., says "I don't like it when you push me"				
Accepts responsibility for own actions				
Understands various family roles, jobs, and rules; e.g., role-plays in housekeeping center				
Follows classroom rules and procedures; e.g., waiting for a turn				

Milestones for Three- and Four-Year-Olds (cont.)

Name: _____

Personal Development	Not Yet	Sometimes	Frequently	Almost Always
Shows interest in discovering and learning new things				
Understands and describes the reasons for his/her actions				
Persists at a task				
Seeks help when encountering a problem				
Shows self-direction; chooses new as well as a variety of familiar activities				
Tries other solutions when faced with a problem; e.g., doesn't give up when unsuccessful				

Physical Development and Personal Health and Safety	Not Yet	Sometimes	Frequently	Almost Always
Uses strength and control to perform simple large-motor tasks; e.g., walks on a line on the floor				
Coordinates movements to perform more complex tasks; e.g., gallops with ease				
Uses strength and control to perform simple fine-motor tasks; e.g., pulls off and pushes on marker caps				
Uses eye-hand coordination to perform a variety of tasks; e.g., puts together large floor puzzles				
Develops control of various writing, drawing, and art tools				
Uses a variety of equipment for physical development				
Follows basic health and safety rules; e.g., carries scissors and pencils with point down				
Performs some self-help tasks independently; e.g., dresses, washes, and dries hands				
Knows how to dial 911				
Knows school fire-prevention and escape plans				

Milestones for Three- and Four-Year-Olds (cont.)

Name:_____

Cognitive Development: Listening and Speaking	Not Yet	Sometimes	Frequently	Almost Always
Listens with interest to stories told or read aloud				
Derives meaning from nonverbal and verbal cues				
Listens with understanding to directions and conversations				
Follows directions that involve a two- or three-step sequence of actions				
Creates rhyming sounds; e.g., *bunny, funny, sunny*				
Speaks clearly enough to be understood by most listeners				
Uses language for a variety of purposes; e.g., ask questions, tells stories				
Initiates and responds in conversations with others				

Emergent Literacy The Individual Profile lists these milestones.

Social Systems Understanding	Not Yet	Sometimes	Frequently	Almost Always
Begins to recall recent and past events; e.g., names a skill they can do now that they couldn't do when younger				
Expresses beginning geographic thinking; e.g., shows location of objects in room on a flannelboard				

Milestones for Three- and Four-Year-Olds (cont.)

Name:_____

Mathematical and Logical Thinking	Not Yet	Sometimes	Frequently	Almost Always
Shows interest in quantity and number; e.g., holds up fingers to show age				
Counts objects to 5				
Recognizes and duplicates simple patterns; e.g., strings beads in repeated pattern				
Sorts things into subgroups by different characteristics; e.g., colors, shapes				
Identifies and names several shapes				
Uses comparative words that show order; e.g., beginning, middle, and end				
Uses comparative words in measuring activities; e.g., *shorter, taller, longer, faster, slower*				
Uses positional words; e.g., *above, below, under, beneath, behind*				
Orders (seriates) several objects on the basis of one attribute; e.g., shortest to longest, smallest to largest				
Constructs a sense of time; e.g., knows that story time comes after nap				

Creating	Not Yet	Sometimes	Frequently	Almost Always
Initiates the use of a variety of art materials for exploration and experimentation				
Participates in music experiences				
Participates in group creative-movement experiences				